Marketing Professional Servi

The Chartered Institute of Marketing/Butterworth-Heinemann Marketing Series is the most comprehensive, widely used and important collection of books in marketing and sales currently available worldwide.

As the CIM's official publisher, Butterworth-Heinemann develops, produces and publishes the complete series in association with the CIM. We aim to provide definitive marketing books for students and practitioners that promote excellence in marketing education and practice.

The series titles are written by CIM senior examiners and leading marketing educators for professionals, students and those studying the CIM's Certificate, Advanced Certificate and Postgraduate Diploma courses. Now firmly established, these titles provide practical study support to CIM and other marketing students and to practitioners at all levels.

The Chartered
Institute of Marketing

Formed in 1911, The Chartered Institute of Marketing is now the largest professional marketing management body in the world with over 60,000 members located worldwide. Its primary objectives are focused on the development of awareness and understanding of marketing throughout UK industry and commerce and in the raising of standards of professionalism in the education, training and practice of this key business discipline.

Books in the series

Below-the-line Promotion, John Wilmshurst

The CIM Handbook of Export Marketing, Chris Noonan

The CIM Handbook of Selling and Sales Strategy, David Jobber

The CIM Handbook of Strategic Marketing, Colin Egan and Michael J. Thomas

CIM Marketing Dictionary (fifth edition), Norman A. Hart

Copywriting, Moi Ali

Creating Powerful Brands (second edition), Leslie de Chernatony and Malcolm McDonald

The Creative Marketer, Simon Majaro

The Customer Service Planner, Martin Christopher

Cybermarketing, Pauline Bickerton, Matthew Bickerton and Upkar Pardesi

The Effective Advertiser, Tom Brannan

Integrated Marketing Communications, Ian Linton and Kevin Morley

Key Account Management, Malcolm McDonald and Beth Rogers

Market-led Strategic Change (second edition), Nigel Piercy

The Marketing Book (third edition), Michael J. Baker

Marketing Logistics, Martin Christopher

Marketing Research for Managers (second edition), Sunny Crouch and Matthew Housden

The Marketing Manual, Michael J. Baker

The Marketing Planner, Malcolm McDonald

Marketing Planning for Services, Malcolm McDonald and Adrian Payne

Marketing Plans (third edition), Malcolm McDonald

Marketing Strategy (second edition), Paul Fifield

Practice of Advertising (fourth edition), Norman A. Hart

Practice of Public Relations (fourth edition), Sam Black

Profitable Product Management, Richard Collier

Relationship Marketing, Martin Christopher, Adrian Payne and David Ballantyne

Relationship Marketing for Competitive Advantage, Adrian Payne, Martin Christopher, Moira Clark and Helen Peck

Retail Marketing Plans, Malcolm McDonald and Christopher Tideman

Royal Mail Guide to Direct Mail for Small Businesses, Brian Thomas

Sales Management, Chris Noonan

Trade Marketing Strategies, Geoffrey Randall

Forthcoming

Relationship Marketing: Strategy and Implementation, Helen Peck, Adrian Payne, Martin Christopher and Moira Clark

Services Marketing, Colin Egan

Marketing Professional Services

Winning new business in the professional services sector

Michael M. Roe

Published in association with The Chartered Institute of Marketing

OXFORD BOSTON JOHANNESBURG MELBOURNE NEW DELHI SINGAPORE

Butterworth-Heinemann
Linacre House, Jordan Hill, Oxford OX2 8DP
225 Wildwood Avenue, Woburn, MA 01801-2041
A division of Reed Educational and Professional Publishing Ltd

℞ A member of the Reed Elsevier plc group

First published 1998

British Library Cataloguing in Publication Data
A catalogue record for this book is available from the British Library

ISBN 0 7506 4127 4

Composition by Genesis Typesetting, Rochester, Kent
Printed and bound in Great Britain by
Biddles Ltd, Guildford and King's Lynn

FOR EVERY TITLE THAT WE PUBLISH, BUTTERWORTH-HEINEMANN
WILL PAY FOR BTCV TO PLANT AND CARE FOR A TREE.

Contents

To the prospective reader

Hello, my name is Michael Roe, and I've written the book you are holding which is called *Marketing Professional Services*. Had you heard of it before you picked it up just now?

'. . .'

Well, that's interesting. You see, the book was designed exactly for people like you, who are offering professional services to their clients, in order to give them a clear and simple framework on which to build a cold canvassing and marketing campaign. I think this would be of tremendous value to you and your organization – and that's why I would like to invite you to browse through the chapter headings in the contents to see what benefits the book can offer you. Would you be free to do this now or would you rather wait till later?

'. . .'

Yes, you're right, there are a lot of books on the shelf around you with apparently similar titles, but what I think you'll find with mine is that it is the only one written by, and focused on, the needs of a professional services provider, and that's why I'd like you to look further into my book – can you do this now or would you rather do it another time?

'. . .'

It may indeed seem a lot of money for this book, but I'm sure you'll agree that, when set against the potential millions of pounds of new business out there to be won, it is excellent value, so would you like to look further now or a little later?

'. . .'

Of course, you're busy right now; I think people are always short of time nowadays, but that's why I just suggested you first browse through it, either now or some time soon – which would you prefer?

'. . .'

Excellent, I'm glad I've persuaded you to have a quick look now. I'm sure you could be equally persuasive on behalf of your own professional service with my help, and would find my book both intellectually and financially rewarding. So let's get started . . .

Acknowledgements

While the initiative, execution and practical experience were mine, the opportunity to learn new business winning skills, to apply them, and then to pass on my knowledge, derive from many helping hands. I acknowledge them all below with immeasurable thanks:

Victor Lewis, MD of World Trade Publications, for introducing me to the world of telesales, to MBA Training, and for constant advice and guidance

Barry Marcus, co-founder of MBA, whose original training course on prospection formed the foundation of my skill base

Research International, my employer, for allowing me the opportunity to apply my ideas and expound them openly in this book

My seminar partners who have allowed me to quote them liberally here, namely Simon Rhind-Tutt, who linked it all together for us using his all-round marketing skills; to Claire Spencer, our PR specialist; to Tom Rayfield, our man in the Agency (and humorist); and to Bill Pegram of PWA.

My family and mother for their love and support.

Introduction

This book comes as a surprise out of another surprise. The author was working for many years as a professional in a services sector then seen as being somewhat academic in mentality and lacking aggression in sales. To be concrete, I was (and remain) a senior market research director who had worked for a considerable time serving marketing clients from my position in a major international research agency. Life had been comfortable, only mildly disturbed by thoughts that maybe more could be done to energize my particular business, and the sector in general.

Awoken by a take-over resulting in a more financially demanding owner, I took the initiative to become better acquainted with a new environment, that of sales and selling. What I found was not only the brash world of salesmanship, but also the subtle, challenging and effective skills of prospection and cold canvassing. These latter techniques seemed surprisingly suitable for transfer into my sector. I asked for and was given the opportunity to apply them. Another surprise – they worked ! And as I became more involved in the selling of my own professional service I realized that we were not even applying the skills of marketing that were the very raison d'être of our major clients. Others I met in similar professions were making the same sort of discoveries about the lack of marketing and sales activity in their fields, whether these were consultancy, accountancy, advertising, design, PR or other comparable professional service sectors.

A few years went by and my own new business success rate continued to build, resulting from a mix of cold canvass sales in particular – hundreds of presentations to prospects leading to millions of pounds worth of new business – and marketing activities in general – which won an award from the Institute of Sales Promotion. It seemed a natural development to tell the uninitiated about it – in my own organization and outside (spurred, I am sure, by a mixture of pride, enthusiasm and egotism).

I linked up with a few like-minded converts. They were specialists in their own fields of marketing, advertising, direct marketing, and PR, and their contributions are recognized in this book at each of the relevant chapter headings. We ran seminars entitled 'Winning New Business' sponsored by Marketing Week magazine . . . and people came ! Professionals like ourselves. Professionals who wanted to win new business, and who wanted to do so by applying skill and judgement, rather than just enthusiasm and luck.

Furthermore, they told us afterwards that they felt they had learnt something valuable and were really grateful to myself and my team. Not from our crude 'close that sale!' or 'do you seriously want to become rich!' exhortations – those were not our messages. But from material we had designed for their own special circumstances. So this book, never intended at the outset, was the next surprising, but logical, development.

What I can offer you, the reader, comes mainly from my own practical experience, enlarged through my contacts with those who joined me in the seminars and by some additional reading. It is a practical 'How to . . .' book, designed for your use and not as a contribution to academia.

Its applicability should extend beyond the UK; I have lectured across Europe without meeting strong 'it'll never work here' resistance. My audiences in the UK have also included some from outside Europe. And common sense dictates that the principles will apply well in North America, the home of salesmanship.

I make no excuses for the constant references and examples from my own experiences within the profession of market research. That's where I tested the theories of winning new business and found that they produced results. So that's where my examples come from – it's what I know best. Just replace the words 'market research' in my sales pitch with your own offer when you read my cases and samplers and it should work fine.

The more I read, the more I realized that most service professionals are alike in relation to the subject of winning new business. You may not be a market researcher or work in marketing services; you may be a consultant, a lawyer, an architect or an accountant. Whatever. We all have intangible services to offer to other professionals. These intangibles are information and knowledge. Too often they remain hidden assets. This must be changed – we must make our target audience aware of our knowledge base so that our new business 'suspects' can move across the boundary to become 'prospects' and then clients. Competition is increasing its clamour for attention, whilst concurrently there is a general feeling among clients that differentiation is lacking between the offers made to them. At the same time our colleagues, fellow professionals, are not as (new) business aware as they should be. So we ourselves must be more active.

There are three ways to lose business – you can lose an existing client; you can have your proposal rejected; you can fail to be invited to tender. For me, the latter is the worst crime, because you have not even got to stage one. This book is about avoiding such a situation.

So much is out there to be gained by learning how to make your presence known to potential clients personally, frequently and professionally using some simple skills in preparation, prospection and presentation; and to build this all around a well thought through marketing plan. That's where my advice can help you. Some adjustment to your own particular circumstances may be necessary. But keep the basic principles in mind, then adapt and apply to market your professional service and win new business.

Good luck!

How to use this book

> The most important single method of developing a practice is through personal contact. It has clear advantages – total flexibility, comprehensive, attention getting'
> A. Wilson (1994), *Emancipating the Professions*, Wiley

Agreed! But how to do it? Seminars were my first means of communicating to a wider audience my practical experience of cold canvass selling my own professional service. My multi-disciplinary group of colleagues and I made up a lecturing team of five, and we constructed a day-long programme covering most of the features listed in the chapter headings preceding. We each focused on our own specialism and attempted to generalize from our specific personal experiences so as to be relevant to the broad professional services sector audiences that we faced. Our aim was to provide a full overview of the subjects of selling and marketing professional services such that delegates would feel that they had received a practical and complete training which they could start to put into operation very quickly.

The day began with an explanation of the logic of the programme, as now described in Chapter 4, which we then followed broadly in the order reproduced in this book. It seemed to work well, the delegates departing full of praise for both the structure and content, and keen to put our theory into practice for themselves. Therefore, it should be perfectly possible for you too to read the book from cover to cover and gain the same benefits as the seminar delegates. The style I have chosen is conversational, based on the lectures, so if you are here for 'the full monty', please feel free to study all the techniques presented from start to finish.

At the other extreme, my own bias and 'specialism' is undoubtedly linked to personal contact, the skills and benefits of prospection and cold canvassing, and, if that is what particularly interests you, I am happy because I think I have something special to offer. In such circumstances, you may wish to dip in at Chapter 5, which represents the heart of the book, and move on from there as your interests take you. Chapter 5 comprises the theory and practice of prospection skills, also providing operational hints and tips and many sample exchanges between service provider and prospect. (The latter replace the real exercises I conducted with the audience using two phones in the lecture room.) After reading the full chapter you can consider yourself equipped to start prospecting for your own organization immediately.

But nothing exists in total isolation, and it would perhaps be more logical for you to take three chapters together as a segment – numbers 4 through to 6 – which includes the key Chapter 5, but adds in the theoretical structure – in the preceding chapter – together with advice on how to cold canvass when you get to your appointment – in the following chapter. These three form a unit, focusing on my 3 'P's of:

Preparation

Prospection

Presentation

You will find multiple sample illustrations of real successful prospection calls and presentation meetings towards the end of each of Chapters 5 and 6, with a concentrated summary of the 3 'P's at the conclusion of Chapter 6. After these, you can explore the other chapters in any order. The choice is yours.

Whichever strategy you adopt, please bear in mind that Chapter 3 and the final chapter cover the broader theory and a practical example of putting that theory into action respectively, and so should not be missed.

Chapter 1

Winning new business – your duty

The lion and the gazelle – a new business parable

Every morning in Africa a gazelle wakes up.
It knows it must run faster than the fastest lion or it will be killed.

Every morning in Africa a lion wakes up.
It knows it must run faster than the slowest gazelle or it will starve to death.

So it doesn't matter whether you're a lion or a gazelle, in new business ...

WHEN THE SUN COMES UP, YOU'D BETTER START RUNNING!

Attributed to Sanders Consulting, 1992

It's a jungle out there! Working in professional services, you may see yourself as being above the life or death struggle of sales, being a 'purveyor' of professional expertise rather than a 'seller' of services ... but nothing could be further from the truth. Unless you win (read, sell) new business you will die like the gazelle or starve like the lion.

My book aims to provide you with life-preserving skills, hopefully life-enhancing ones too. It is based on the premise that new business is the life-blood of all commercial activity, no less so in professional services. And it stresses that the duty of getting this new business is yours. If your job

description includes the words ' new business', 'business/practice development', or 'marketing', then there can be no doubt about the book's relevance
to you. But whatever your job involves – fee earner/consultant/partner –
you are billings and profit responsible and it is vital that you start now to
commit to business generation. You and your firm's business life depend on
it, so you cannot avoid your duty.

My aim is to help you generate lots of new business (as a solus activity
or alongside servicing existing clients) . . . in other words, to sell successfully.
But I am not a salesman myself. I am a professional servicing the marketing
industry, like you the reader, I am a professional selling to other professionals. What I am is a professional who has been bitten by the new business bug
and who determined some time ago to pursue my objective using a little less
luck and rather more skill.

Professional skill. Because the objective is to add a third professional
element into the equation: to *professionally* sell professional services to other
professionals. The noun 'salesperson' doesn't sit comfortably in this context
– but the verb 'sell' must never be avoided. No salesperson, however brilliant
at his or her craft, could ever replace you in front of the client, because he
or she would not possess the professional qualities that remain vital in the
above situation, namely in-depth professional services training, skill, experience, and knowledge. You do not sell from a rate card. The client expects to
talk to you as an equal in professional competence. In fact, the people to
whom you're selling are so similar to you that in many cases the roles could
be, or already have been, reversed. Sellers switch to being buyers and vice
versa all the time.

You may not wish to be a salesperson, considering yourself a practitioner,
but you should not be snobbish about the salesperson's skills. They are finely
honed and you would be foolish to ignore them . . . just as you would be
foolish not to apply them without some sensitivity as to the professional
nature of your prospect (you are not a double-glazing salesperson) . . . just as
you would expect to add them to other professional marketing skills, some
of which may be your own basic stock in trade: advertising, PR, direct
marketing, etc.

Those already in marketing are familiar with the fact that most of the
classic mnemonics start with 'P'; the same applies to the winning of new
business. In fact, there are three Ps here: prepare; prospect; present. By
employing all the above-mentioned skills, this is what you should achieve –
lead generation, appointment getting, and then arriving face to face with the
prospective client. Not surprisingly therefore, the core Chapters 5 and 6 of
this book focus on prospection and cold canvassing, the centre of the new
business process.

Why should the face-to-face presentation be so vital? Well, what you are
selling is an intangible, a service. And when it comes to selling intangible
products, or indeed product intangibles, there is one guru. He is Ted Levitt
of Harvard Business School from whom two quotes are relevant:

'the product will be judged in part by who offers it'

'people use appearances to make judgements about realities'

Harvard Business Review, May–June 1981

What this makes clear is that **you** are the tangible representation of your service, the main judgement criterion. All the rest is trust – you are the reality on which the prospect will have to make his or her judgement. As well as representing your agency/consultancy/partnership, you also differentiate it – you are the most distinctive element, the unique feature. So, you must present yourself to the prospect along with your service.

Halting a moment on this issue of 'trust'. A US consultancy, Synectics Inc., has spent a considerable time determining what impacts on trust. In fact they have developed a formula for it:

$$TRUST = \frac{CREDIBILITY \times INTIMACY}{RISK}$$

It is the correlation between 'intimacy' and trust that is particularly relevant here. It confirms the need for the face-to-face interaction that forms the core of this book. 'Credibility' can be built through other marketing activities, 'risk' is related to the spend of the client and so usually out of your control (although the plus point for professional services is that often a low cost trial of your organization is possible before a major commitment is necessary.)

This book will, however, cover the full range of sales and marketing tools available to you. Their employment (or deployment) will be based on your own specific new business needs evaluation coupled with marketplace judgement. A full-time commitment is recommended (from its earliest days, the original Saatchi and Saatchi Advertising Agency had always used a dedicated team working on new business which did not divide its time with another job.)

Can you/your firm afford this? It may not always be possible, particularly in the case of a very small consultancy. But full time or part time one thing is clear – you will need to devote **quality** time to new business. Because always remember – investment will be rewarded. A skilled and effective prospector/ cold canvasser should return gross margin equivalent to well over three times his or her total costs.

And enthusiasm. It is only through a combination of skill and commitment that you will be successful, only through this combination that you will overcome the basic fear of selling. Make no mistake – it is really fear that produces what masquerades as superiority over the lowly salesperson; fear of rejection, fear of failure, fear of raising your head over the parapet and shouting ' buy me!'.

Philip Kleinman, reporting in *ADMAP* magazine on a meeting of the Association of British Market Research Companies (ABMRC), noted:

'an interesting question put to the audience was how many of their
research agencies employed someone whose principal job was
getting new business. Out of 28 firms, only 5 said they did'.

So why not take inspiration from some people who can be admired without
reservation for their professional skills, and yet who placed **equal** emphasis on
selling skills. They are drawn from the world of advertising, and represent
three generations of success within that world, from the classic ad man, David
Ogilvy, via the next generation Saatchis (first time round), on to the 1990s new
wave, Rupert Howell of HHCL.

Ogilvy: 'Your first duty is to get new business.'

Saatchi: 'Our new business department is the account handling
department of all the clients we don't yet work for.'

Howell: 'There is no magic (new business) formula – just a system,
energy, and resources.'

Campaign, February 1991

Why did these ultimate professionals place so much emphasis on the selling
function? Could it be that they all appreciated the 'leaky bucket' theory of
running a service business?

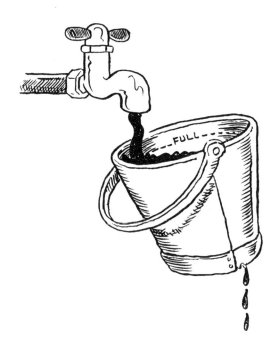

Your business can be represented by this leaky bucket; your objective being to keep the bucket full of water (read, business), indeed full to overflowing, the overflow representing profit, the water level representing work-in-progress. But the bucket has a hole in the bottom. Try as you may, you cannot completely plug this hole. It does not necessarily represent unhappy clients. There is a multitude of reasons why today's live client becomes tomorrow's lapsed client: budget cuts, absence of suitable briefs, personnel changes, etc. There are a number of ways you can attempt to reduce the diameter of the leak: contractual business, client maintenance programmes (see Chapter 11), etc. Yet there is one unavoidable solution: opening the tap above the bucket and letting the new business flow in, continuously.

The danger is to see this as a short-term measure – a quick fix (see Chapter 3, item 2). If you truly believe in new business then you will realize that the only way to proceed is to consider every existing client as vulnerable and new business as a constant need. Your working hypothesis will be:

> 'however busy I am today, I must sell now for tomorrow.'

Wait until you are less busy, with time available for selling, and by definition you'll be too late; by the time your emergency actions take effect, you'll be out of business.

When reviewing the sad decline of Colletts Advertising Agency, John Spearman was quoted by *Campaign* magazine as follows:

> 'In my day, we anticipated a loss of 20 to 25 per cent of billings a
> year, and therefore we needed new business. You are foolish if you
> do not work on that assumption'
>
> *Campaign*, March 1992

Your client base is fluid. Probably, like my own analysis year on year, your client tracking will reveal two crucial facts:

1 one-third of last year's top twenty clients are not in this year's top twenty;
2 year on year, 10 per cent of clients disappear from your list, 40 per cent spend less than before, 50 per cent spend more, so it is the new business alone that drives growth.

What greater incentive than this sort of analysis can there be to drive home the selling message? The need is clear, the skills available (read on!) – but is there a motif, a commonality that distinguishes selling marketing services from other kinds of selling?

In my view there is, and it can be simply represented.

All clients think they have unique problems, are special

and as a result they buy 'a la carte, only rarely off the shelf, because they're looking for their own solutions.

The professional services supplier understands this and has the answer:

'I can help!' This is the motif that permeates every page of this book – 'your problems are unique, my solutions are customized/tailored to meet your needs.' After all, if I cannot help you, what am I doing here in the first place?

Another US academic, Warren Wittreich, quoted in the *Harvard Business Review*, put the matter most succinctly. Referring to the business of selling a service, he stated three rules:

> Understand problems
> Offer the professional
> Minimize uncertainty
>
> *Harvard Business Review,* March–April 1966

If you really can help ... and if you can sell ... then success is assured. In this book I am telling my story because the skills and techniques espoused in the following chapters WORK! They are not part of arid theory, but living, practical, working methods that have and will deliver results. That's why many chapters contain a case study. There are actionable tips on every page.

And remember, while you are wondering what to do and how to do it, your competitors are likely to be mounting assaults on your clients. The downside of working in a service industry is that you're only as good as your last job. Quoting Ted Levitt:

> 'Satisfaction in consumption can seldom be quite the same as earlier promise. Once sold the customer can easily be unsold as a consequence of underfulfillment of expectations. Customers usually don't know what they're getting until they **don't** get it!'

Back to the parable of the lion and the gazelle: if you're not up and running, they're going to get you.

You must: identify with the client's view, differentiate your agency by getting yourself in front of the prospect, and then overcome obstacles and sell.

To stay with the 'help' motif, how can this book help you to achieve new business? By remembering all along that 'you' are a professional first, a salesperson second; and by remaining thoroughly practical in giving guidance. No grand theories, just passing on to you what has worked for me. There may be some 'Golden Rules' stated – in fact, they represent advice rather than dogma. The case studies reveal how they work in practice.

Chapters 2 and 3 start the whole process off by providing the overview: everything you ever wanted to know about new business but were afraid to ask. Following chapters go into detail on specific elements, so that eventually your new business arsenal should be ready and primed.

After that it's up to you! The time for excuses will be over, you'll have to go for it. Banish fear. It may or may not be true that some clients put a notice in reception:

> We shoot every third salesman
>
> The second has just left

You'll know this doesn't mean you. You're still a professional. You're there to help. Go for it! It will work. Let's rather end with a few up-beat quotes; the first comes from Andy Welling, then marketing director of Commercial Union:

> 'I work in an industry famous for having to sell its products. I expect to be sold to. Being sold to is a way of gathering information and I don't object to it. I enjoy it.'
>
> *Marketing*, March 1993

The second, from an anonymous advertising agency CEO referring to his search for a business development director:

> 'I would be prepared to fund a package plus incentives that would enable the person I want to earn comfortably more than I do, just as long as they get us on to pitch lists. If anybody in my position thinks there is another means by which they can stimulate new business then they are out of their mind.
>
> *Campaign*, November 1992

So, clients have the budget; service organizations the need – let's get the two together. Only fear is keeping them apart. If you apply the skills of this book, you can be the catalyst to bring them together for the benefit of both.
     Finally, another manner of visualizing the situation in our sector – HIPI:

> H = heterogeneity; a service is not homogeneous
> I = intangibility; a service is not tangible
> P = perishability; costs continue whether or not you have work
> I = inseparability; the client is always part of the deal
> Riley and Long, *Characteristics of Selling/*
> *Buying Professional Services*, University of Lancaster

I interpret this as further support for my exhortation for you to get out there and meet your prospects! Your professional service USP, especially when personally presented by you, represents the heterogeneity referred to above, acting as the tangible link with the client, without whom the business would not be there – and then you may indeed perish!

Chapter 2

The role of marketing inside a professional services organization

'Marketing – the management process responsible for identifying customer needs and meeting them profitably.'

Chartered Institute of Marketing

This book is about winning new business through selling. I want you to achieve the sale, reap the success and the rewards that go with success, including the pride that you did it yourself. But it is made abundantly clear in the next chapter that selling must be placed within the context of an overall plan, and such a plan is likely to be a marketing or business plan. Marketing involves much more than selling alone, and an overview of all the elements is provided below. The plan must be robust, well thought through, fully justified and, of course, costed. Such a plan is essential to ensure that the entire marketing effort and, within it, the selling function, is taken seriously and receives the necessary commitment from the very top of your organization. Without that commitment you will be pushing water uphill the whole time and will lose your own, necessary motivation. Yet with it, you should receive adequate resources of time and money that are perceived by all your colleagues as an investment rather than as a cost, and you should feel confident that everyone is aware that no quick fix is being attempted but rather a long-term effort. (You might think you have everything to gain from a short-term 'fix', but in fact selling takes time to show results and a long-term commitment is in your own interests.)

The book is also predicated on the assumption that you, the reader, are actually the very professional whose services are on offer to clients. That is the position I myself was in when I started, and it is from such a base that my own successful experiences are based. This book then attempts to assist you in grafting, just as I did myself, new business generation sales skills via cold canvass onto those professional skills, so that you can win new business *through your own actions*. I was a market researcher – I became a market researcher who could sell. You are a 'professional' and you can become a 'professional who can sell'. As far as I am concerned, the other elements of the marketing plan are simply there to provide more prospection leads to aim your selling activities at, and to lubricate the sales process.

However, in some (often larger) professional organizations the need for a business development function has now been accepted at the highest level, and a staff appointment made. The title often becomes 'marketing' or 'business development'. The appointee may be an internal one or an external, often marketing, specialist. Such specialists are frequently drawn from the world of fast-moving consumer goods (fmcg), the birthplace of marketing – but are often unfamiliar with cold canvass selling! There is a danger that prospection and cold canvass efforts will be relegated to the back of the list, behind those activities (PR, advertising, etc.) with which the appointee has greater experience. This book aims to provide an antidote to such an attitudinal deficiency.

In the case where you are going out to sell for yourself, the skills expounded here can be directly applied. They are designed and explained for you to employ immediately – and to claim the credit when they produce results. Of course, you are quite at liberty, and may wish to, act additionally or solely as propagator of them throughout your organization. The material in this book should enable you to motivate and train others. It is further possible, as mentioned at the end of Chapter 5, to subcontract the prospection aspect of the cold canvass process to an outside agency, although I think you should have a go yourself first, because there are risks, as well as costs, relating to contracting out.

In the case where you are not a professional in the sense implied in these pages, then you *must* act as a 'centre of excellence' covering all marketing and sales skills. Obviously you are not yourself able to be a direct business getter via cold canvass since you do not have the professional qualification. But please do not ignore the power of cold canvass. Propagation of the techniques expounded in this book should become your main task, within the context of a total marketing plan, the formulation of which and your direct involvement in other aspects of which were obviously the *raison d'être* for your appointment. This role is not an easy one, since you are neither a professional nor a fee generator – and so are perceived as an outsider and an overhead – plus a nuisance and a hard taskmaster in your attempts to turn unwilling profession-als into direct salespersons. This can lead to much resistance and sniping, requiring you to develop considerable political skills to fight back and justify your position.

The tensions and difficulties of this situation are best followed in the pages of the excellent magazine *Professional Marketing* (published by PM International, London) where marketing practitioners in professional service organizations agonize over their role and status. It all boils down to the necessity of your justifying the effectiveness of professionals becoming salespersons themselves and of you yourself as a 'staff' overhead expense (see Chapter 6: Rewards) alongside 'line' fee earners who feel that they are the real bulwark of business and client relationships. As a result, you must add to your task the role of coach/educator/inspiration to those around you. When it comes to the use of PR (Chapter 7), its first target will be internal! You will have to ensure that all in the organization sign up to the broad goals expounded in the plan, which includes your cost! Resistance comes from those who feel – 'we have got on well enough all these years without marketing/canvassing, so why do we need it now?' The answer is clear – your company may have performed reasonably well to date without these activities, but it sure as hell will not be able to continue to carry on that way without falling seriously behind target and competition.

If you are fortunate enough to be on the board, you will not fail to notice the barbed comments aimed in your direction, as those with direct profit/fee income illustrate their own achievements without looking in your direction, yet clearly imply wonderment at the little you have contributed. This can become even more frustrating when you know that they have, often unconsciously, employed some or all of the elements forming a part of the techniques espoused in this book – and transmitted via yourself – but are unwilling to admit it! Cold canvass is the ideal vehicle to help you to fight back because it provides a direct link between cause and effect – 'that job you won – do you remember who visited them last month?'

Whether you are doing the selling activity yourself or motivating others to do it, always see it in the context of 'the marketing plan' (next chapter) and believe in its ultimate success! Remember, marketing is not just about how to get brochures done! In fact the process should include all of the following:

- **Winning new business**
  within which, cold canvass is the clear leader; few other marketing tools can so directly generate business, although direct marketing can get close.
- **Understanding your market**
  your own knowledge of your market gained from experience and contact with actual and potential clients; but also capable of enhancement through the objectivity of market research to allow a real SWOT analysis.
- **Building your brand**
  corporate identity, advertising, PR, literature, sponsorship – all are the brand-building elements of the total marketing mix, together with visibility at conferences, seminars and exhibitions.

- **Planning your strategy**
  the business or marketing plan – make sure you have a role in its construction
  and that it finds its way onto the board agenda, with a defender present to argue
  for it.
- **Managing existing clients**
  quality deliverables through quality processes via ISO systems, plus satisfaction
  monitoring.
- **Marketing internally**
  internal communications and training.

It should – but does it? A research study conducted by McCallum Layton for
Wheeler Associates in 1997 ('Marketing the Advisers') produced some
worrying conclusions from their interviews with 100 leading business advisory
firms, reported in *Professional Marketing*. The study's sponsors themselves were
sufficiently worried to make the following comment on the marketing function
(where it existed at all!) within these organizations:

> 'Most content themselves with looking after marketing
> communications – PR, advertising, the corporate identity and
> publications. Few currently have a mandate in the client management
> and new business areas.'

I worry not only about this but also about the fact that cold canvass was not
mentioned at all in the entire document. I hope you will make sure that you are
not restricted in a similar way. The report went on to recommend:

> Employ at least two marketing staff for every 100 fee earners and
> spend at least UK£2000 per fee earner on marketing.

The definition of marketing as provided in the heading to this chapter is precise
but brief – it must encompass new business which in turn must, in my opinion,
encompass cold canvass for a professional services organization. Every profit/
fee earner must become involved and so have a stake in marketing.

A feature of marketing speak is a focus, some may say obsession, on market
share. Do you know your market share in your particular professional area,
and subsectors within it? It is revealing and motivating to try to calculate it,
because it is usually very small, mostly in single figures. Now look at the
reverse of the coin – how much there is to go for out there; how much in
turnover you could gain if you only increased your own share by one
percentage point! Surely not beyond the bounds of possibility? Marketing and
selling will take you there.

Chapter 3

Running a successful new business programme – twenty golden rules[1]

In this chapter, I shall stay on the broader issue of the overall strategy before moving the spotlight onto the individual tactical elements in later chapters. But first a reminder on a key issue – the competitive framework.

I don't know if you are able to remember a famous old Pepsi ad which filled the TV or cinema screen with a babble of linking adjectives also shouted out on the soundtrack until you begged for a pause . . .

lipsmackin,thirstquenchin,acetastin,motivatin,etc,etc.. . . .pepsi!

Well, that's just what the professional services Tower of Babel is like. Promotional messages are being aimed at your prospects (and clients) at all times on all media, in the office, when travelling and at home. You probably think of your competition as being, at the very most, others in your particular

[1]Based on lecture material from Simon Rhind-Tutt of The Tutt Consultancy

sector. But, take the target's viewpoint and I have found within marketing services alone:

adagencies,prcompanies,salespromo,directmarketing,sponsorship,graphicdesign,
packagingdesign,salesincentives,corporateentertainment,consultants,charities,
salesbrokers,typesetters,trainingcompanies,commandersalesforces,marketresearch,
media,presentationcompanies,fringemedia,productplacement,referralagencies,
strategists. . . .etc,etc,etc

Yes, it's bedlam out there. Noisy!?! I asked a marketing director to collect all the mailings she received in a typical month and it filled a crate. Literature in all shapes and sizes, from postcards to full colour glossy brochures, from free samples to letters almost begging for business, from announcements of upcoming conferences to offers of help from individual freelancers, and so on. And then add the trade and professional magazines that land on the desk with their advertising and tip-ins, the insidious Internet ads you cannot escape as you browse, the telephone sales activities, and so on. How are you going to make an impact in an environment that is so busy?

Well the first step on the path to getting through the noise is to acknowledge that it is there. Too often marketing plans seem to be constructed in a vacuum without any attention being paid to the noisy environment within which they will have to function. There seems to be an assumption that the prospect is sitting quietly at the desk just waiting to hear from you and able to give you all the attention you need. So the message becomes diluted, the print small and dense, the reasoning rational – is it then a surprise that months later few of your prospects can recall receiving anything from you!

You too must shout. You too must fight for attention, aim to be remembered. Your plan should be formulated to cope with a crazy, noisy surround. You have to queue jump, you can't always be polite. If you hang back, someone else will step in and take your place – someone with a worse offer than yours but with a louder more strident tone. And your message must be a simple, clear, differentiated offer.

1 Plan

If you fail to plan you will be planning to fail

The new business 'fire' (see below) should be part of an overall business or marketing plan. Seems obvious, and the issue has been raised in the previous chapter, but so often it is not done. It is something both you and the whole company should be involved in, but with principal focus at the chairman or managing director/partner level. And the reason is simple – their involvement is a sign of genuine commitment.

This will also ensure that adequate funds are available. Because, while never forgetting the element of skill to which this book is totally dedicated, there remains a clear correlation between resource investment and success in the new business arena. A study by the IPA (Institute of Practitioners in Advertising) looking into the amount of resources that were going into new business for all the advertising agencies within the organization revealed a figure of 5 per cent of turnover for the larger (and faster growing) agencies against only 2.6 per cent for the smaller ones.

New business should be a part of the corporate business plan, which targets clients and market segments, and addresses the particular services within the company portfolio that are the profit generators and therefore require sales actions in support.

To sum up, there is probably good sense in the following quote from Ambrose Bierce's *Devil's Dictionary* with regard to the value of planning:

> '. . . it is the best method of accomplishing an accidental result.'

On the other hand, I am a strong believer that a plan is no more than a statement of intent, with accompanying budget – it cannot and should not be required to detail the creative execution. It can be as elaborate as you like in its review of the current situation, its analysis of the requirement, its statement of objectives, its commitment to the marketing philosophy and allocation of time and money to the process – but at this stage you cannot be precise about what you will do and how it will look.

Putting the plan into effect will require liaison with the creatives to find a way to execute – to decide between the media, to create the headline, to discover the 'hook' and the 'look', to develop a rational and emotional message that moves on from the offer you have to the benefit to the prospect, etc. This is a venture into the unknown – and equally as exciting and equally as unpredictable. Don't promise a creative outcome to yourself or your board; it will come during the process, and you must ensure they understand your inability to define it at this stage. Yet, if the plan is right you should be confident that the execution will be also.

2 Create a fire, you can't flick a switch

Here are some wise words from a past new business director at the Young & Rubicam advertising agency in the USA:

> 'New business is rather like building a darn good fire. You need to start off slowly, gently nurturing it, and not expect results immediately. With constant care and attention, the fire will grow and grow and the investment of logs instead of kindling will produce

> even greater results. The fire can now burn freely and produces
> great rewards. But beware, if it is left unattended for any length of
> time, you can be left trying to resurrect ashes.

For so many people new business is thought of as a light switch – 'we've got a problem, so let's just go out and get some more jobs; right, that's worked, so forget it for now, it's all hands on deck to cope with the business we've got.' And so the seeds of the next crisis are sown.

It is a classic cycle of – urgent need, short-term action, some results, so let's get back to normal – oops, problems again! Not surprising really. A quick fix provides the volume and the relief from business slow-down, but this very volume increase will result in your personnel being overloaded, which, coupled with no real commitment to the sales activity anyway, allows it to be easily dropped again ('we're too busy to sell'). Then it will not be long until the problem re-emerges.

My message is – keep selling; no matter how busy you are now, there is a dip in the road up ahead somewhere. In fact, in the professional services area particularly, it is just when you are at your busiest that it is most likely that you are finishing off a large number of projects and will very shortly raise your head and wonder where the next one is coming from. Then it is too late to kick-start the sales activity because the warm-up time takes months, during which period you could become bankrupt! So insist that the marketing and sales activities run through continuously regardless of the success or otherwise of your business and the pressures on your staff. Keep your internal sales and marketing meetings going through those periods when the participants say, with superficial logic, 'I can't attend, you shouldn't ask me to, I'm too busy working on the business our own activity has already generated'. This is a danger signal; insist that it be ignored.

3 Investment of time as well as money

When existing staff are being asked to stretch their job description into the new business arena, the time element becomes even more relevant than money. They must be given the time, and on a regular basis, to invest in new business activities. It should be a weekly task, maybe daily. It is quite independent of individual workload or corporate successes/problems. As stated above, keep going even when business is good. It needs to be on the agenda all the time, with action reports passed up the line on a regular basis. Prospection and cold canvass in particular eat up time and nervous energy. It is always easy to find something superficially more immediate to do. Don't allow this to happen – to yourself or to others.

If your operation uses time sheets, then it would be a good idea to have 'new business activity' or 'sales and marketing' pre-printed on the record form so that the importance of the function is in front of everyone continually. Allow for it in your target setting of billable time, record and present results to all colleagues. Do not allow carping of the kind 'well of course X has been doing a lot of selling – his business is going belly-up and he's got nothing else to do; my own area is such a success I've no time for roaming around prospecting'.

4 Treat your company as a brand – research it and define it

What is a brand? Well, the Chartered Institute of Marketing defines a brand in this way (with my own interpretation in italics) – it must have among its target prospects:

- A clarity of perception
  Your organization should stand for something – a USP (Unique Selling Proposition) with which you are permanently associated and which you make your property; it underlies everything you do and say and can be sensed, directly or indirectly, in all your communications.
- A positive perception
  It may seem trite and obvious, but have you checked that your USP is both unique and appealing? Too often the claim does not produce the anticipated perception among prospects – instead of 'yes, I need them' it becomes 'oh no, not another', relegating you to anonymity.
- A level of differentiation
  Always ask yourself whether your offer and its communication are really distinctive; too often they are bland, boring and indistinguishable from the competition.
- Reach or spread
  Your aim is to get to the maximum number of prospects (and existing clients) for the minimum expenditure. Different media should not overlap too much but should rather be able to extend your reach.

So stand back and look at yourself – you are a brand in a highly competitive market and you must consider:

- **Clients and prospects**
  - *Who are your target audience?* – Define your target universe in terms of business sector, level of seniority, degree of sophistication, familiarity with your specialism, geographic spread, etc.
  - *What are their real needs?* – Remember the principles of market segmentation: markets are becoming more and more fragmented and it is growing less and less likely that one offer can satisfy all. You may need to divide your services into specialist or niche subsectors each of which will be targeted at specific client needs segments.
  - *Who do they use?* – Know your competition. What are their strengths and weaknesses; how would you answer the question 'why should I switch to you?'

- *How do they choose?* – What is the DMU (decision-making unit) within your clients' organizations? Who gets involved in the process, who makes the final decision? Who has a veto? Who signs the purchase order? Where do they get their information from?
- **Competitors**
  - *How do they operate?* – Do their services compete directly with yours or are they coming from a different professional framework and so position themselves differently (possibly also applying another pricing policy).
  - *How do they present themselves?* – Construct a competitive dossier: collect all advertising, direct mail and PR materials you can (use a friendly client to help).
  - *How are they positioned?* – Analyse the competitor information; look for the philosophy: it may not always be overt in their material; pick their publicity apart and try to isolate their marketing strategy.
- **You**
  - *Where do you want to be in relation to all this?* – I come back to a number of points I made earlier – you must have a USP, be differentiated, and your actions will have to stand out from the noise. Develop your strategy in this context.
  - *What are your strengths and weaknesses?* – Conduct your own SWOT analysis and then consider: is your best path forward seen to be by capitalizing on your strengths and dominating in this sector, or rather by eliminating your weaknesses and so bringing in a new growth area (It is often too heavy to do both of them at once).
  - *Does this mean radical changes?* – A change of direction may require new staff, training existing staff, designing new offers, etc.
  - *What are the implications for your new business investment?* – You may need to delay a marketing blitz until all the above are in place, tried and tested.

If some of these questions cannot be answered, and even if they can, it can only do you good to invest the time and money necessary to gain an objective insight – via market research, of course! Research your own market thoroughly. Even consider researching your own staff to see if they see their own company in the same way as you and your clients do. Use an outside consultant/agency to gain objectivity. See Chapter 13 for more advice on research usage.

5 Marketing is more than new business

What the above really means is that you should have a marketing strategy, not just a new business plan. Such a strategy should be based on the strong foundation of research evidence, not hearsay. So the information requirement listed above should be professionally and rigorously gathered.

And this marketing strategy should include existing clients too. There's nothing worse than producing exciting promotional material aimed at potential new clients and forgetting to circulate it to your existing ones. It goes without saying that existing clients are still going to be your mainstay and must never be sacrificed on the altar of new business.

Some of your own staff will not be motivated by the new business or even by the marketing process. That is not a crime – as long as they do not denigrate those who are active. And vice versa. There should be a place for both in the organization. Those who keep a major client happy year in and year out are of incalculable value and must be allowed to stand in honour alongside the new business winner – a successful company rewards them both. But you must gently remind the business retainer that their business should not stand still and will be budgeted to grow, since there is an even greater chance of gaining new business from an existing client than there is from a new one.

6 Develop a clear vision

Are you satisfied with the status and position of your organization as revealed through your research? What are your strengths and weaknesses? What type of company do you want to be?

The first place to start is to develop a clear mission. This is necessary to give a focus to both management and staff, and to be translated by marketing into a message for clients too. It should be obvious to anybody who comes into contact with the company exactly what you stand for. Claim the high ground and tell everyone about it – internal and external. So even if key personnel are out of the agency and decisions have to be made by others, there is a guideline because there is a vision defined.

Of course, the mission needs to be credible, and in this context it will need regular review and possibly updating as the company develops. New business strategy must be a part of it.

However, too often mission statements are pure motherhood and offer no real distinguishing features – 'we want to be the best', 'we aim to be number 1', '. . . to increase shareholder value', etc. If the chairman must have this, then let him, but insist that somewhere the needs of clients are addressed. A wording of the type 'we aim to be the first choice for XYZ services among all those clients with the need for ABC thanks to benefits offered by our unique LMN' can be directly translated into marketing and sales actions. It can almost write the headline of your advertising, the punchline of your direct mail and be the focus of a cold canvass call.

7 Aim high – but make sure you've got a safety net

'Reach for the stars and you won't get a handful of dirt!'
Leo Burnett

Setting objectives should follow this credo. If you're comfortable with your target then you are probably not pushing yourself hard enough. The target should be ambitious but achievable, and everyone should buy into it. New business is about living on the edge, continually trying to better yourself, always looking to see just what is possible.

But the unanticipated or blockages may occur, and there should be a reserve in case expenditure needs to be increased (competitive action, an unexpected promotional opportunity) and a fall-back position if financial pressure means a budget cut, or if one element of the mix is not proving effective. The plan should be broken into segments or sales periods that are regularly tracked and assessed. There must be budgetary controls.

Prospection and cold canvass planning means setting target numbers and then keeping good records, probably on a weekly basis, of performance:

- How many contacts achieved?
- How many pitches made?
- Comparison with previous week/year?
- Quotes issued (by value and volume)
- Strike/conversion rate?

... but have a safety net! Build in a contingency. Don't let the viability of the company depend on hitting the top of your target. Be practical and sensible as to how the new business strategy is incorporated into the financial plan. The motto is reach for the stars, but not blindly such that fractionally missing your target puts you out of business. 'All or nothing' has no place in this world. Nor should you listen to competitive gossip and adjust your plans in the light of booze-inflated new business figures bandied around by competitors in the pub!

8 It's better to do a few things well than many badly

The key word here is 'focus'. But focus can mean one of two things – focus of message and focus of timing. Focus of message means beaming the correct message to the correct audience. It may also mean keeping on message, i.e. ensuring that your message or messages are still part of a uniform whole which projects a single company image that meets the mission statement objectives. So break your plan into clear segments and define exactly what each segment is supposed to do. Whatever happens, keep to this target, while not neglecting all the tactical moves you will have to be making in response to daily events. It may not be possible to do everything at once, the money won't be there. So keep focused.

Focus of timing is less easy to legislate for. Don't overlook synergy – two simultaneous activities are probably better than sequential equivalents, since promotions interact and feed off one another in a geometric manner. But do you want to commit your entire budget in one big bang and then disappear off the radar screens for the rest of the year? Obviously, you may want to avoid the summer and Christmas holiday periods, but do you really wish to join the crowd in the autumn when everyone is likely to be active? Given your own resources are likely to be limited, the sensible starting point is to aim for a spread of activity across the year, with synergy coming from message uniformity rather than from a blitz of activity at one particular period.

9 Remember the competitive framework

Yes, I know this has been said before, but it deserves repeating. Everything you do will be released into a noisy world. So be creative, be different, be loud, and be professional. This is not a warning or a plea – it is a must. If not adhered to, your message will drown, and your marketing budget with it.

And consider professional help. You can't be an expert in everything. It is a false economy to do it all on the cheap, in-house. I know you can write a good line, may even be able to draw a bit – but that doesn't make you creative. Nor does it make you objective. An outsider can reveal new insights and create a revolutionary approach that will really impact and shake up the market.

10 Treasure your database

This is absolutely vital in order to track prospects (and indeed your clients). It is amazing how few companies have a good database and, even if they do, how poorly they use it (very often its use does not extend beyond the Christmas cards!) It should be a repository for information on each client and provide the basis for a regular and meaningful contact with them, i.e. the heart of a communications strategy.

I am not the person to recommend the ideal software to you. The offer is enormous, experience varied, evidence of good practice almost negligible. No one is happy. But one thing I can suggest is – don't be too ambitious. Size is not everything! It's what you do with it that's the key. It's much better to have a small active database than an enormous macho one that lies unused and unloved. Because a good database requires a major effort just to build it and then constant tending to maintain it – it is always out of date. Who's going to do this? It makes one hell of a difference to the resource required for this whether you are dealing with hundreds or many thousands of records.

But the last thing you want to do is to starve your database of the information it requires to be effective. Keep reminding your staff (and yourself) to enter updates on existing clients monthly. After every new business prospect call, every meeting, every pitch, there must be a contact report and information added to the existing record or a new one set up. It is never-ending. It is a responsibility that should not be delegated. It is too easy to pass the task on to an office junior who will, through no fault of his or her own, simply validate the familiar maxim of 'garbage in, garbage out'. Only those directly in contact with clients or prospects can have any chance of confirming the data is correct, spotting spelling mistakes, remembering that article in the trade press announcing the company that has moved office or the client that has moved company.

Custom made or off the shelf? Current software developments allow almost anyone to build their own database very easily nowadays. But the advice again must be to consider the use of a professional list in addition. There are many purchasable databases around. They are not perfect (assume 15 per cent is going to be out of date before it even reaches you) but they offer you the opportunity to spend your time going out and making contacts rather than being stuck on the telephone laboriously trying to identify each contact from your own list of companies. If you buy, don't be seduced by numbers, buy no more than you can keep up to date.

Finally, protect your database. It's valuable and horribly mobile. Back it up all the time and lock it (physically and via passwords). To lose so much effort would really be a crime, in more than one sense.

11 Don't be afraid to test

Don't be afraid to test new ideas. Marketing theory is all built around the principle of pre-testing since the financial commitment and risk involved in mass marketing is enormous and demands small-scale evidence as a precursor to major expenditure. In the professional services arena, numbers are smaller in absolute terms but not relative to turnover. Many of your proposed activities are amenable to small-scale, toe-in-the-water trials to evaluate response before a full commitment.

This can particularly apply to mail shots, which can be pre-tested on a small section of a mailing list and reactions monitored. The mail cost is small, so is the print run. Any damage caused by failure can be restricted to a few tens of clients/prospects. Similarly, if you want to use a new presentation approach during cold canvass, why not simply test it out during the next few presentations?

For advertising, company identity and literature, the commitment has to be all or nothing. This does not prevent you going to a sample of clients/prospects with unfinished material and determining their response to it – does it communicate? Is comprehension satisfactory? Does any element require clarification, removal, explanation? Accept the results – even if it 'kills your own creative baby!' It is sometimes hard to take criticism on a creative approach you believe in and have spent weeks or months developing. But the customer is king; accept the verdict and go back to the drawing board – your next idea will be all the better for it.

12 Use all the tools of the trade

Marketing is multifaceted. It offers a wide range of tools for placing your offer in front of clients and prospects. These tools comprise:

- **Cold canvassing** – *prepare; prospect; present (face-to-face)*
- **PR** – *free publicity! Yes, but only if you work at it*
- **Advertising** (including sponsorship and the Internet) – *paid-for publicity*
- **Direct marketing** – *not just direct mail*
- **Print material** – *company literature*
- **Conferences, seminars, exhibitions and training** – *placing your skills in front of an open (subscribed) or closed (invited) audience*

I want you to use them all – each for the right purpose, with the right objective, at the right time, for the right target group. I will deal with them individually in more detail later in this book, with special focus on prospection and cold canvass, which in my opinion and experience should be the jewels in the crown. A typology linking them is provided in the following chapter.

Let's not forget tools that I have consciously NOT included. The first is telesales. It is important to stress the distinction between telesales and prospection via the telephone. The former is designed to close on a sale, the latter to close on an appointment. The skills used in achieving both have elements in common, but the intrusion factor is quite different. In the marketing of professional services, I espouse the latter and consider the former unworkable, alongside 'free sample' or 'special introductory price' offers.

I have not included client entertaining. I see this as an area in which I have little new insight to offer. Obviously it has a lubricating role in the sales process with existing clients – I don't see how it can work for new prospects without entering the murky area of bribery!

13 Invest in your own training

Winning new business is a complex activity, it comprises so many different elements, as shown above. Don't think you can or have to do it all yourself. Neither you nor your staff can be experts in all of them. Nor will you have the time to devote equally to all these different aspects of the new business process. Train yourselves in what you keep in house. There are more than enough books and seminars which aim to allow you to become your own PR specialist, copywriter, seminar organizer, etc. This book itself fulfils part of this function.

But you will still almost certainly have to buy some services in. I suggest you buy in (or contra deal, see below) what you cannot do yourself and what you can afford. But consider very carefully before buying in services that will come into *direct* personal contact with prospects. You wouldn't hire an agency to entertain your prospects for you (taking them to a restaurant on your behalf!)

– so consider very carefully whether or not, for instance, to use an agency to cold call them using your name to make appointments. These services exist but opinions differ as to their ultimate effectiveness.

14 Consider contra deals

Within the above constraints, hire professionals for that which you cannot do yourself. Specialist agencies can seem expensive, and cheaper alternatives may come to mind (ironic, considering you would not like your own clients to think that way about your own profession). The expense of using outside professionals may be mitigated by the possibility of contra deals with your advisors, e.g. you design their brochure in return for them giving you PR services, you do their accounts and they do your market research. When using freelancers the same may apply, e.g. they do your newsletter in return for utilizing some of your facilities.

But, on the whole, I recommend you go for quality despite the expense, because you will end up with the best value if they achieve what they should – a spectacular, creative concept.

15 You can only initially sell a meeting

It is highly unlikely that any of the marketing activities listed in point 12 above will of themselves directly close a sale. Nor should that be your objective. In professional services it just doesn't work like that. The aim of it all is to get you in front of the prospect – see Chapters 5 and 6 – hence the focus on prospection and cold canvass.

The tools are a means, not the end in themselves. They are being employed solely for the purpose of getting you to that all-important first meeting. Advertising is sexy, design is pretty, PR is 'absolutely fabulous' – but keep the purpose in the forefront of your mind: 'I want to meet that person!' You want to meet them before your competition does, and it will undoubtedly help if that meeting takes place against a background where the messages you want to convey are likely to enter a brain already prepared to receive them thanks to the preparatory, softening-up work achieved by your marketing actions.

16 Work hard at press relations

In some ways this is a better term than public relations. You need to form a relationship with the journalist(s) with whom you are dealing. The people that journalists really listen to and take notice of are the people that know their medium. They need you as much as you need them – so create a two-way process – see Chapter 7. They want copy and should come to see you as a source that offers reputable and knowledgeable comment and content. In your turn, you must not be a time waster, gaining instead a reputation for delivering relevant and supported material at the right time and in the right format for them to be able to use.

This is all time consuming, particularly as your contacts will always want to talk to you personally, so delegation will be difficult. Furthermore, you're in for the long term if you want to maintain a constant profile – which should be your aim; you can never assume you are well known. The benefits of publicity can be considerable – so be available, and without regretting the time it takes.

17 Prepare, prepare, prepare

You had a business development plan; you fought hard to get it accepted; you spent money, time and effort in the execution of your strategy; it comprised many elements . . . but really there was one and only one aim and that ultimate objective is in front of you at last – the meeting with the prospect. You don't want to blow it now! You will in all probability only get this one chance. So prepare yourself, and those who may go with you, in terms of what you will want to present, how it will be presented, and the answers any questions. (The practical details and your strategy for the meeting are dealt with more fully in Chapter 6.)

Don't plan to rush the presentation. Ask for sufficient time. Don't think of yourselves as representing an intrusion – the client has needs, problems requiring solution; you are there to help. Use your time allocation to the full.

But don't just plan your side of the meeting – be prepared to listen as much as to talk. Clients like to tell you their problems, so listen and adjust your pitch to answer the needs that are raised. Be flexible – the meeting is not yours, however much you are determined to focus on your pet subject. The client's agenda is the only one on the table. Follow it for success. If you insist on sticking to your own programme you will become an intrusion and the 'help' factor will disappear.

In the practical arena, obviously confirm the meeting and all details in writing beforehand. Then do your homework; using published information, store/site visits, existing agencies, etc. And cast your team as detailed below.

As to the meeting itself, make it one for the client to remember! Not for your pratfalls but for your professionalism and creativity. Know the judgement criteria. Ensure you offer help, answer the brief, and meet those criteria. If necessary, rehearse your presentation – don't ever feel you are sufficiently prepared.

18 Cast the right team

When you get to the object of all your activity, that face-to-face meeting, whether it's the first presentation, a beauty parade, or a later pitch situation, always think of the personnel that go to make up your team. You are the casting director with the aim of achieving bonding with your audience as soon as possible. People buy people, and it's your job to cast your staff such that they will get on with the potential client. Some of your people are performers who can add that up-front 'magic' to your pitch that will tip the balance in your favour; others are best left in the backroom where they are equally valuable, but in a different way.

The individuals you select must be enthusiastic and enjoy working together – it will show. They should not outnumber the clients, except if the client is alone, in which case I still feel that there should be two of you (as a safety measure in case the chemistry of one does not seem to work; and to get two evaluations after the meeting).

19 Keep in touch

This is more difficult than you think. How often can you follow up and say 'Hello it's me; how's it going then?' or 'Gissa job!'

On the other hand it's no bad thing to appear hungry. So you need to find a catalyst, something new, something interesting which you can send or use as an excuse for a phone call. And don't forget that all your other marketing activities are out there working for you as a constant reminder of your existence – your PR, advertisements, direct mail, etc.

A letter of thanks, addressing points that might have been raised during the meeting, is an obvious necessity. But what else, or what next? Before going into the meeting you could already have had in mind an item you can use as a follow up. You may have held something back, a technique, a piece of literature, etc., which you can then send on with an 'I thought you might be interested . . .' note.

20 'People give business to the people who really want their business'

So, always be thinking of that little bit extra.

Perseverance and tenacity will always be rewarded, especially if accompanied by flair. Don't expect results overnight, but do expect results. It is quite possible for a new business 'seduction' to be successful two or more years after the first meeting – and such delayed consummation is all the sweeter!

These, then, are the twenty golden rules referred to at the start of this chapter:

1 Plan
2 Create a fire, you can't flick a switch
3 Investment of time as well as money

 4 Treat your company as a brand – research it and define it
 5 Marketing is more than new business
 6 Develop a clear vision
 7 Aim high – but make sure you've got a safety net
 8 It's better to do a few things well than many badly
 9 Remember the competitive framework
10 Treasure your database
11 Don't be afraid to test
12 Use all the tools of the trade
13 Invest in your own training
14 Consider contra deals
15 You can only initially sell a meeting
16 Work hard at press relations
17 Prepare, prepare, prepare
18 Cast the right team
19 Keep in touch
20 'People give business to the people who really want their business'

But there is a good excuse to move on to number 21. After all the chapter title includes the word 'successful' and that is what you will be. When this success comes it is very important to CELEBRATE! For your own motivation, for the team, and for the future and many more new clients.

There will be enough low morale moments along the way to need cancelling out on those (happily) regular but (unfortunately) fleeting occasions of actually winning. Yes, there will be days when nothing seems to go right, when you can get through to no one, when your PR release is ignored by all media, when part of your mail shot comes back with 'moved one year ago' written on it. Winning new business more than compensates for it all.

Yet even those moments of achievement are fleeting because within that split second the target has been transformed from a distant object of desire to a demanding 'current client'. You now have to deliver. And to move on to the next prospect. Guaranteed the win has come just when you are having a hectic day, a key staff member is on holiday, or the computer network is down. As you drown under the pressures of daily work, the wonderful memory of the successful chase and capture rapidly become distant. So do celebrate, however briefly.

A quote from Lord Saatchi

At the beginning of this section I stated: 'And your message must be a simple, clear, differentiated offer'. Then I repeatedly stressed the need for you to develop a mission, a USP, clarity of perception. Lord Saatchi, one of the original founders of Saatchi & Saatchi Advertising, now onto his second agency M & C Saatchi, has put this issue even more succinctly in an article in the *Financial Times* (January 1998). While his focus was on global consumer brands, I think the message applies to all levels of business.

'There is a straightforward mathematical test (for your brand anatomy). It operates on the basis of a word count: in your brand strategy, how many words describe the characteristic you are trying to own?

In each category of global business or species, there are only a few emotions that drive human being's purchasing decisions. These emotions will be available for ownership by one brand or another. But in any global business category, it will be possible for one brand to own only one emotion. And some of them have already been booked.

The mathematical test counts the number of words in your strategy. It forecasts sea changes in the future to a maximum of 12. One, two, or three words, and the changes you are likely to face will be little wavelets and ripples; eight or more and you are facing gales.

The lesson is that if you stand for a certain emotion you will have people for you and people against you. But if you stand for no emotion, or too many emotions, you will have nobody for you and nobody against you. You cannot survive.

So pick one characteristic your brand stands for, own it, know everything there is to know about that one emotion, all over the world. Express it simply, do not dilute or complicate the message.'

Chapter 4

The elements of business development

All the tools of your trade as new business generator for a professional service were revealed to you in item 12 of the previous chapter – cold canvass, PR, advertising, direct marketing, print, exhibitions and conferences, training and seminars. The next step is to provide you with an overall plan and then a detailed description of how to employ each of them, to show how they interrelate, with examples and case study material giving practical evidence of their effectiveness. Some of these tools are for you to use yourself, others may require the help of outside specialists. Some are vital, others are optional. Some are expensive, others are cheap. All are a means to an end – to get in front of the prospect and present your professional services: the cold canvass.

In this context it is useful to have a classification system for these varied options. Consider the following metaphor, which aims to aid your visualization of the different objectives and to illustrate the effects of each element. It is not a perfect illustration but it is designed to help you keep the purpose and contribution of each in context.

As a NASA probe, PROSPECTOR 1, moves deep into the darkness of outer space, 'the final frontier', boldly going where no man has gone, so you embark on your sales campaign. NASA and you both believe that there is intelligent life out there (in your case prospective clients requiring your services), and are prepared to try a range of methods to establish communication. Both the probe and you are in a region of darkness, attempting to get in touch without damage to either party. You hope for a 'soft' contact during which both parties will learn something to their mutual advantage.

The means at PROSPECTOR's and your disposal to achieve a successful mission may be classified as follows:

- **push**   *probing for life at the furthest boundaries*
- **pull**   *tempting life forms to identify themselves*
- **expand**   *keeping the probe supplied with fuel for onward motion*

What do I mean by each of these three terms? Let's start with 'push'. Here communication is outward and the probe is sending its message on a number of different frequencies, not having any real idea which wavelengths can be received by the life forms. The probe attempts to announce its presence to the widest potential 'audience', taking a 360-degree target at the maximum reach, and a 'one-to-one' at the minimum.

The latter, the most focused, narrowcasting element of this push metaphor is represented by 'prospection', my favourite tool. This is a face-to-face communication attempt, where you have identified the prospect and are focusing much time and effort in achieving personal contact, without any advance promise of success. Prospection should lead directly to cold canvass, and the way to achieve such an end result is explained in Chapter 5. This direct link between cause and effect, between prospection and the cold canvass (see Chapter 6), makes assessment of its effectiveness easy and cost benefit analysis straightforward, as long as the time you spend is put into the equation realistically.

On a broader band comes 'advertising', spreading the message across wide swathes of the universe with more hope than likelihood of impact (see Chapter 8). Nowadays this should include a consideration of the potential value of setting up a web site. Sponsorship is another form of advertising, where the medium is the message since there is little room for the message itself. Evaluation of effectiveness is more difficult for advertising. Usually you have to rely on intermediate measures such as awareness surveys, unless a direct response mechanism is incorporated. Sponsorship has the same limitation, while web site 'hits' and 'visits' are easier to quantify.

And finally, 'PR' represents the ultimate in broadcasting using a wide transmission, with the possibility of penetrating the tiniest nook and cranny in the universe, albeit with low signal power (see Chapter 7). It achieves this by stealth, hiding the sales message among universal call signs. This makes determining its effectiveness even harder to assess than for the other elements. But it can claim greater authority and no one doubts that it can be successful.

Moving on now from 'push' to 'pull'. Here the stimulation of in-bound communication is the aim. Life forms are being 'tempted' to identify themselves, and more than that, even to give away the full co-ordinates of their positions so that they can be contacted again. The only hope you have of achieving this is to become so sexy and attractive that a response is enticed. In other words, by making them an offer they can't refuse. This represents the role of 'direct marketing' – generating response through an offer (see Chapter 9).

The aim is to get the life forms to reveal themselves because they cannot resist. So direct marketing requires an attractive offer – without such an offer it remains 'junk'.

Also in this category should be 'print material'. Such a classification may seem unusual and controversial, so the reader is referred to Chapter 10. Put briefly, it is not company brochures which are being dealt with here but other company-produced print material which is put on offer to prospects and which, because of its interest value, should generate a response. So we are, in fact, talking about print material becoming an element of your direct marketing.

And finally, expand. Now I am stretching the metaphor to its limits. Let's assume our probe has a power source to maintain its flight further and deeper into the unknown. While the push and pull activities are going on, it is still essential to maintain the probe's forward momentum. In short, fuel supply is required. Equivalent to getting more business out of your existing clients. Expanding the existing franchise. It is after all the existing clients that are providing the income (fuel) that keeps your organization afloat and finances (fuels) the new business effort.

Key elements in this exercise are conferences, seminars, exhibitions and training (see Chapter 11), print material (as described above), and pro-active client servicing. All these are designed to add fuel to the engine. The former show the benefit of using words such as 'fuel'; 'keep talking' could be the motto, don't lose contact or the motor will stop turning. The pro-activity could be spontaneous proposals for new activities, suggestions for syndication, etc. It should also include a serious review of cross-selling opportunities, which is the equivalent of burning the same fuel twice over by getting the very maximum exploitation out of each of your existing clients.

By deploying some or all of these means, push/pull/expand, the probe will certainly track down the life forms – just as you will identify and win business from your prospects. Precisely which prospects will turn out to be the fruitful ones is as impossible to predict as is the whereabouts of interstellar life. But it **is** out there, and if the messages are transmitted continuously and consistently then a response will eventually be achieved. Furthermore, when all the elements of exploration work together and produce a momentum of curiosity, the message will start to work its way around to other universes as the 'beings' converse with one another – and then that most tenuous (but real) of all communication media starts to work for you, whatever the alien equivalent is of word of mouth.

A case study that features most of the elements I have referred to is provided at the end of this chapter. Its interest lies in the deployment, in an integrated manner, of the full range of available options and reveals their immediate and long-term success, eventually in more than one market environment.

As always, a key aim of all these elements is to identify prospects. After the case study come Chapters 5 and 6 which form the core of the book, elaborating and instructing on the main 'push' factors of prospection and cold canvass.

Chapter 7 and beyond deal with the other aspects of the marketing mix. But not as individual treatises; there is more than enough literature already available on how they work. My focus will be to show you how each of them can assist in the main prospection/canvass push.

There are two ways in which they play their roles – lead generation and lubrication. I will emphasize how all push and pull marketing elements must contain response mechanisms. As a result, prospects are encouraged to identify themselves and now become leads for your prospection and cold canvass work. When you make contact with them, the second role of push and pull marketing should be able to manifest itself. If the prospect has seen, heard, or received your marketing material he or she should then be in a more receptive frame of mind to accept your approach. This is the lubrication role. So together, the marketing elements smooth your path to cold canvass sales success.

A multi-element case study
The relaunch of a professional service business

Background

Market research – a professional service sector within the marketing services industry staffed by university-trained professionals wanting to be treated as consultants, like McKinsey. A project-based business requiring constant pitching to maintain income flow. Average project size is around £30 000 and lasts 3–4 months. But variability is huge, with £5 million, three-year long contracts also possible.

The large market research agency Research International (200 staff) was, at one and the same time, an old and a new kid on the block in the early 1990s. Old because it had been in existence for over twenty-five years; new because for most of that time it had been a division of Unilever and traded under its original name, RBL.

Small, aggressive agencies (sometimes focusing on specific problem areas: staff numbering from 10–50) were making life difficult for the newly titled Research International, which had recently gained a new owner.

Its history meant that RI was a large agency (£20 million turnover) but with a somewhat reactive rather than proactive style. The image of the company (RBL/RI) was of high quality, but at a high price. Staff were considered good problem solvers and good all-rounders, but poor at speedy, responsive customer service.

'A sleeping giant' was the way some described RBL/RI. 'A tortoise with a top hat' was how it was more commonly typified – and the hare was outpacing it.

Analysis

A new generation of top management, with a revitalized board, was determined to reverse this situation. The aim: to boost sales via the launch of an integrated marketing strategy, utilizing internal resources and supported by professional help.

A market research study among clients and potential clients soon revealed:

- Awareness of RI was still below that of RBL.
- In either case, spontaneous (top of mind) awareness was very poor, despite good prompted awareness:

	RI	RBL	Competitor
spontaneous (%)	10	15	24
total aware (%)	80	72	95
'too expensive' (%)	23		
'does not respond quickly enough' (%)	14	N/A	

(client telephone survey, 150 respondents)

there were signs of some shift in the client profile for research in general, with a new, broader base of less regular, younger buyers with needs that varied from occasion to occasion. Of these, 79 per cent did state that they sought advice before commissioning research.

- Access to RI was difficult: 'so many experts, but who do I ask for?'

As one summed it up: 'RI , the largest unknown research agency in the country!'

Strategic implications

A marketing director – myself – was appointed from one of the existing board team, as a full-time position. I signed up an advertising agency, JWT Direct, a PR company, Handel Communications, and a design agency, ADC Design. (Note: none of our competitors employed a dedicated marketing director or seemed to have a professional marketing strategy.)

It is easy with the benefit of hindsight to make history more logical than was actually the case. The strategy development about to be outlined below represented the happy confluence of a number of initiatives, some of which were already underway before the marketing review exercise began.

Two of these need to be noted now. First, I had a little earlier started functioning as a new business director, focusing on sales and running a major prospection and cold canvassing campaign with considerable success. I had achieved 100 presentations in a year using the technique described in the following chapters, but needed more leads. Second, the company was already toying with some of the print material options detailed below.

There now came a crucial moment when the analysis given above, having been translated into key objectives:

1 'To make RI famous ... get on prospects short-lists'
2 'To match the complexity and range of the RI offer to the explosion of need from the new client base; to make the agency accessible'
3 'To win new business'

was followed by a brainstorming session between advertising agency and company at which a solution emerged that itself became the motif for the entire integrated strategy.

That solution was the HELPLINE. If one of RI's key problems was inaccessibility, then a telephone hotline would surely be a valuable solution. At the same time it would be innovative, memorable, and useful; in fact a classic example of 'pull' or response marketing (see Chapters 8 and 9) generating new leads for prospection.

But much more than that. It was soon obvious that the HELPLINE itself could be a seed for many spin-off marketing actions. It would indeed act as a symbol of the new RI, representing the agency's problem-solving capabilities and its ability to put its size and experience directly at the disposal of its prospects and clients. Other initiatives already in gestation were seen to fit well under the same 'help' motif. Publications particularly.

The company was planning two publications: first, a series of monographs each relating to a specific research issue; second, a booklet featuring abstracts of all conference and seminar papers given by RI personnel over the previous twenty years. These, it was realized, also offered help to prospects and clients, being reference documents rather than brochures.

Implementation

The full pull/push range of techniques was featured in the relaunch of RI.

- **Prospection and cold canvass:** already in full flow, and planned to maintain the strike rate of 100 presentations to new prospects a year.
- **Advertising:** comprised two elements, the second of which could also be termed direct marketing, the key aim being to generate a response.

Prior to the launch of the HELPLINE, which would, of course, feature the RI name, it was felt that some action should be taken directly to address the demise of the previous, but still salient, RBL title. A single execution was therefore placed in the trade journal of the research industry to 'kill off' RBL.

'Three characters from Research International have gone missing – RBL'

was the headline.

Now attention turned to the launch of the HELPLINE (*see the advert on page 36*).

This campaign was featured in the research, marketing and advertising trade press with a total spend of around £50 000.

- **PR:** the launch of the HELPLINE coincided with the hiring of a PR agency. It presented them with the perfect vehicle to bring the new RI to the media's attention. The HELPLINE became a media event (it was indeed stressed that the service also offered benefits to journalists).
- **Direct marketing:** obviously the HELPLINE itself was an instrument of direct marketing 'pull'. Its presentation utilized the response instrument.

The core element of the launch advertisement was the 'logo' on the front of the telephone drawing, which contained the entire HELPLINE message in a space of 115 × 75 mm. This was converted into a sticker of which 25 000 were sent to targeted

HOW CAN YOU PREDICT YOUR BRAND NEW IMAGE? CALL THE HELPLINE!

RESEARCH INTERNATIONAL HELPLINE
071 823 2636
Market research advice . . . call direct to a director.

Call 071 823 2636 and talk direct to a director of Research International about our unique LOCATOR micro-modelling technique. We'll help you shift your brand-image data from descriptive to predictive. And we'll help you use the data as the basis for multinational advertising campaigns.

Find out about LOCATOR free and without obligation any weekday between 9.00 am and 6.00 pm with just one phone call to our Helpline.

RESEARCH INTERNATIONAL UK

prospects, and later another 20 000 dropped into an edition of *Marketing* magazine. It was also used as a tip-in on some media adverts.

- **Print material:** RI launched the already-mentioned monographs under the title 'Position Papers'; four initially, but soon rising to ten and then twelve in number. These were produced to a high standard of finish and only pushed RI techniques tangentially. Their main aim was to be useful to research buyers and to be 'collectibles', not 'junk mail' (see Chapter 10).

Similarly, the book of abstracts, known as the *RI Digest*, was mailed to all members of the Market Research Society (around 6000.) Its helpfulness was that it contained the offer to send, free of charge, the full paper of any abstract to any enquirer.

Results

1 *Short term*

Repeating the telephone research survey just four months after the HELPLINE was launched, revealed RI spontaneous awareness almost doubled at 19 per cent. For the HELPLINE itself, spontaneous awareness stood at that time at 27 per cent, with prompted awareness of 47 per cent.

Within nine months, a total of 230 calls had been received on the HELPLINE, i.e. an average of six per week. Eighty-three per cent of these were from the designated target group, and, as a direct result of this contact, with follow-up calls and visits to the new leads, research proposals were written to a value of £1.5 million. At that time £650 000 of these had been converted into actual business from clients that included Tupperware, Saatchi and Duracell.

Within a short period since mailout, ninety-three calls had been received by the RI librarian with requests for papers from the *Digest*. The Position Papers were enthusiastically received, though their distribution was limited to individual hand-outs/mailings.

Considerable word-of-mouth response indicated the impact of our marketing exercise. Relevant people noticed that RI was active. Probably equally satisfying was the response from competitors, who were quoted to say: 'we're green with envy', and 'a smart idea'.

2 *Long term*

The demand for the HELPLINE indicated that this would become a permanent service offered by RI. Similarly, the Position Papers remained to be exploited further, and plans were made to maintain a steady flow of new topics that they would address. PR coverage gradually filled a scrapbook, as RI became **the** source for industry comment. In almost all marketing trade features, RI achieved a dominant 'share of voice'; OTS (opportunity to see) were calculated at 5.27 million for a full year.

RI itself was achieving tremendous new momentum as a company, and its profitability trebled year on year (admittedly from a low base), and continued to move ahead by double-digit percentages in later years, allowing the company to sail through the 1990s' recession totally unscathed. Cold canvass was bringing in well over £1 million a year (see next two chapters) – so the combined integrated marketing strategy was a major contributor to the total company progress, with gross margin income exceeding expenditure (direct and indirect) by a factor of up to five. It was quite clear that RI was now top of mind for receiving research briefs, that it was getting on all relevant short-lists, whereas previously it had been back of mind.

Finally, the HELPLINE launch received two commendation awards at an Institute of Sales Promotion ceremony.

Developments

The original launch advertisement for the HELPLINE was further developed during the following year to feature specific topics. Keeping the same basic visual, the headline was amended to state, for example, 'How much will your new product sell? Call the HELPLINE'; 'How can you predict your new brand image? Call the HELPLINE'

A major extension of the scheme took place a few years later. It was clear that the Position Papers represented an attraction, but their existence was virtually unknown. The decision was taken to feature them all in a new advertisement titled 'What's your position on this?' Readers were offered any three of the papers free of charge if they were buyers of research ... and the response mechanism was to phone the HELPLINE. In this way the 'order' would be taken by a director who could 'consult' with the caller and attempt to fix a canvass visit (*see the advert on page 39*).

The response has been and continues to be huge: 1000 calls per year are being received. While entailing a major mailing, the company could be sure that the papers were going to targeted recipients. As expected, call records proved to be perfect leads database material for more cold canvass, since they registered callers' names, addresses, job titles, telephone numbers, and (via the request itself) areas of interest.

Therefore all 'pull' and 'push' elements of the original new business programme (cold canvass, PR, advertising, print and the HELPLINE itself) remain active today – the best testimonial to their success. A web site is the latest addition.

International extension

Being an international organization by definition, other units within the RI Group were keen that the lessons from the UK should be learnt and applied elsewhere.

The cold canvass process, as defined in the following chapters, has proved to be capable of wide application across Europe and North America, after my own training

course had been utilized.

The HELPLINE idea was extended to three other European countries with success, and the Position Papers were used on a global basis and proved equally popular (translated in some, but not all, locations).

I personally had the opportunity to check out on a second occasion in a different environment whether the success of an integrated marketing strategy could be repeated. In the mid-1990s, a crisis arose at the Brussels office of RI Belgium. The chairman of many years became seriously ill necessitating his absence for half a year, during which period the agency fell into disarray and business levels nose-dived. The fifty-plus staff had been generating a turnover of around $8 million but profitability had been below RI norms for many years beforehand.

This had been explained away on the grounds of tough competition and low prices existing in the Belgian market coupled with the difficulties of finding new business in a small country (population: ten million) with a saturated research business. Here was an opportunity to check out whether this was the truth or a smokescreen covering a lack of proactive sales pressure.

At first sight the situation seemed comparable to the UK – it was agreed that the company had poor awareness, had no sales/marketing plan, and senior staff felt that the hypothesis of market saturation needed confirmation. So, it was agreed to launch a prospection and cold canvass campaign, supported by the launch of the HELPLINE and the use of the Position Papers.

Two years and hundreds of cold canvass presentations later the company had doubled its previous best-ever profit margin and shown a sales growth of 40 per cent. As a reminder of what might have happened had no action been taken, there was one particular month when the company achieved best-ever monthly sales – despite the fact that the number one client historically had spent precisely zero!

Chapter 5

Getting there! Prospection

A Spanish proverb: 'The saints did not pray to God to learn what to do, but for the courage to do it'

The heart and soul of your new business programme should be prospection followed by cold canvassing: taking the actions required to achieve the end-result of placing yourself in front of the prospect – face to face, one professional talking to another professional. At this point your message/offer gains full exposure while under your direct control and with the undivided attention of the relevant potential buyer. Success (almost) guaranteed.

In Chapter 1, the three Ps of winning new business were enunciated: Prepare, Prospect, Present. Here the first two of the three Ps will be further developed, with the presentation (or pitch) covered in the next chapter. It is my general experience that my audience's difficulty lies not in **being** there (presenting) but rather in **getting** there (prospecting)! They are confident that, placed in front of a 'qualified' (i.e. relevant) potential client, they will make a good showing. In fact, they relish this opportunity and would willingly pay for the chance. But gaining the appointment represents a fearsome prospect that requires courage. So this chapter will focus on appointment getting, or Prospecting, in order to take away the fear and show how it is possible for anyone to achieve, given training and the motivation to be in charge of your own destiny.

How to put yourself in front of the client! You, the concrete reality of your intangible professional service. You, who differentiates your service provider from your competition.

Why is there this difficulty with prospecting? Where does the reluctance come from? Probably because it goes against the grain of your 'professional' culture. As a professional you distance yourself from the 'huckster', expecting instead that your services will be adopted for their own intrinsic worth. Pushing them seems to demean their value. And professionals don't beg! Even more so, professionals don't like to be rejected, and you think it most probable (a terrible fear) that your appointment-getting efforts will be rebuffed? Isn't it more honourable to be pursued than to pursue? The answer is 'no'.

This negative mentality is an irrational and intolerable hindrance. It must be replaced by a desire to proselytize: 'I've got a tremendously valuable service to offer, and you will be grateful to me for coming to tell you all about it. 'Why not put yourself in your prospect's shoes; can he or she really be doing their job properly if they are not open to new ideas, services, suppliers? Can there be such a thing as a blinkered buyer of professional services: 'my current agency/supplier, right or wrong.'

So the next step is to overcome your fear. Convinced of the justice of your cause you determine to attack the market. You prepare your credentials presentation, you isolate potential clients ... and then what? How to make the appointment? This clearly involves exposing yourself to potential rejection – and it is frightening.

The solution is available and is presented in the body of this chapter. It is simple and useable by all. It rests on one clear premise: prospecting is a skill like anything else, and the skill must be learnt, absorbed and then applied. It is not easy. Courage is demanded; the courage to raise your head over the parapet and say 'buy me.' You can, however, rest assured that it works. Because, although ...

YOU WON'T BELIEVE IT – IT IS TRUE

though ...

YOU WILL THINK YOU CAN'T DO IT – YOU CAN

though ...

YOU WILL THINK IT UNNECESSARY – YOU'LL BE WRONG

As stated in the opening chapter, you are a professional doing business with other professionals. To keep that business coming in you should be selling. And if you are going to be selling, you owe yourself the benefit of doing it using professional skills. Only by this means will your selling be effective. Believe me, once these have been adopted and are working effectively for you there will be no gap in the smooth transition from preparation via prospecting through to the presentation/pitch, as client after client falls to your message with few, if any, of them being aware of the skill of your method of cold canvass. They will not feel imposed upon but happy to have found an excellent new supplier. That will be your reward for overcoming your fears: the first 'high' of getting the appointment; the second 'high' of an excellent meeting of minds between you and the client, and the final 'high' when it turns into business – new business, your business – and is acknowledged as such throughout your organization.

But for now, the risk seems too great to you – the risk of failure in your efforts, the risk of rejection, the risk of being seen as different from your colleagues, of taking time away from existing business onto new business with an unknown chance of success. Consider instead the risk of not selling – the risk of an existing client being seduced away by the competition, or having a budget cut, or of a change in personnel leaving you without your favourite contact.

So be prepared to change your attitude. Back to the three Ps. Let's take them in logical order . . .

I Preparation

Or, to be crude, leads. Where do you find them? How do you qualify them? How to quantify them? Follow the Q × 2 route – Qualify = ensure that they are in the target group to buy your services; Quantify = has their organization the budget, i.e. is the suspect a prospect?

If you are starting from scratch, you may yourself, or with all your colleagues, be able to construct a lengthy and even quite detailed list of individual names and companies you want to approach. Constructing a wish list is not difficult at the early stages. You know your market, you read the trade press. But remember, the list must be long – no fewer than 100 to start with, so as to give yourself a broad target to aim at and to allow for the high proportion of non-effective contacts that you are bound to face on your first contact attempt. You can never have too many leads. In my own experience, and I am confident you will find the same, the early fear of the prospection process itself, which is initially seen as the main stumbling block to getting up and running and actually winning new business, is very quickly replaced by the desperate quest for more and more leads as your list shrinks.

So a purchased database may be an additional or alternative starting point (already mentioned in Chapter 3). Many are available for sale, of variable quality. Then there are the directories, CD-ROMs, and there is always the Internet. But leads can come from anywhere and everywhere – network as hard as you can, keep alert as you read the press, keep your eyes open as you travel. (I have picked up a long list of interesting company prospects simply by touring business parks and noting the sign boards, or by writing down the names featured on chauffeur signage displayed at the arrivals halls of major airports; then it's back to the office and time spent with directory enquiries.)

My purpose in this section is to provide some more creative lead-generation suggestions that may be useful when the first, more obvious leads run out, and to indicate the philosophy and practice in developing the individual items within any list to the point where active prospecting may begin.

The trade press must be regarded as a prime source for targeted leads. In articles and features individuals are named, interests revealed, problems specified and personal likes and dislikes spotlighted. You will undoubtedly make use of these. Yet there is another section of such magazines which can provide an additional fruitful source of potential contacts; namely the Situations Vacant pages. Here you will find clients clearly specifying their future plans and requirements as part of a job description for new staff. It's often all there: company name, address and telephone number; job title and reporting structure; and, crucially, a detailed job specification which may indicate quite clearly whether this person will be in the market for your services.

In many cases the job title alone is sufficient. The following examples come from the marketing world:

'New Product Development Marketing Manager'
*must be interested in our market research model for evaluating the
sales potential of new products*

'Marketing Services Manager'
this title is known often to incorporate market research purchasing

'Point of Sale Manager'
very likely to be interested in promotions research

Sometimes the body copy gives you all the clues you need:

'Junior Product Manager'
including market and competitive research

'Appeals Executive'
moving towards database marketing

'Product Manager'
will involve liaison with sales promotion and design agencies

Of course, these represent long-term leads – it may be three months or so before the appointee is in place. A strike, say one or two months after appointment, is likely to be very successful, given the 'new broom' mentality of most of those in new functions.

To be honest, this approach, though indeed very effective when applied, suffers today from the high proportion of recruitment agency ads, which are generally anonymous regarding the ultimate client.

The recommended procedure nevertheless is to file away all useable job ads, and at a suitable moment approach the switchboard and attempt to identify this individual.

In making such an approach, whether in the above situation or indeed in trying to identify any lead, the switchboard can be a great ally. A major element of the Preparation phase is simple hard slog on the basic homework of getting the name and title of the prospect. Often this begins at Directory Enquiries to find the phone number of the company itself, and can from there lead you a merry chase to locate the actual workplace of the target. Then the switchboard takes over, and when that is exhausted, it generally pays to go direct to a secretary or assistant in the relevant department.

It is sometimes surprising just how much information is freely given away to help you in this vital, background process. I anticipate that companies will tighten up and give instructions to switchboards not to answer these sorts of questions. While the situation continues you had best exploit it to the full. You move straight on to qualifying your lead. There is no reason at all for limiting your preliminary questioning to the switchboard only; press on as far as you can with the staff surrounding your ultimate target and you should be able to confirm or refute the subject's area of responsibility, budget control, reporting path, etc. All vital information prior to launching your attack.

Obviously your target must be qualified and quantified: the person with the money, the authority and the need. But what if there is more than one? Where then do you direct your aim?

Once again you will have to fight the natural tendency, unfortunately only natural because it panders to your innate fear, to aim low. Start with the juniors you think, they'll be a softer, kinder targets. Wrong! The golden rule is to aim high. It must be obvious that you are after the real source of power and that you should not shirk your duty in addressing it. Go for the CEO, the managing director, the marketing director. No limit. As a sop to your fear, be consoled with the certain knowledge that you will probably succeed even if you fail.

What this cryptic last comment refers to is the 'trickle down' effect of aiming high. Given the application of the prospecting skills about to be presented to you in the next section, there is a high likelihood that your approach to the senior person will succeed. Even should it fail, the probability remains that you will not be repulsed but rather passed down the line. This leaves you in a very strong (in fact, almost unassailable) position with the next contact since you will be able to use the senior's name as a reference for your contact! Who can afford to override their boss?

This semi-accidental trickle-down process is a reminder of another key lead-generation means that is often overlooked (though not by the salesperson) – referrals. Having repeatedly talked of prospection as a part of the 'cold' canvass process, it can now be made clear that all your efforts should be directed at making as few as possible of your approaches from the 'cold.' Instead 'warm' prospecting and canvassing is the ideal to be aimed at: a prospect with whom you already have some common ground; usually a name you can drop. Instantly this raises the temperature from cold to warm and makes the whole prospection and canvass effort smoother, easier, and more likely to succeed. Cold calling is the sharp end of prospecting and is addressed in this chapter; if you can succeed in this environment you will find 'warm' prospection an easy task, even pleasurable in comparison. So why not learn how to increase the proportion of warm contacts in your hit list? The approach you will use will be the same for both – it is simply that your nerves will be less frazzled and the chance of success even higher.

Achieving warm contacts, referrals, is only a matter of having the courage to ask! The time to ask is at the completion of the presentation itself. Therefore the topic will be mentioned again at the end of that section. But the impact starts with prospection so let me quote one classic use of the method.

In the market research world, two key buying sites can be isolated: inside the client company (whether a research manager or marketing personnel directly); at the advertising agency (usually the planner.) Their relationship is often complementary, although ultimate power tends to rest with the budget, which is mostly in the client company. Nevertheless, both parties are often involved in research commissioning decisions. Such a situation provides fertile ground for the referral system, particularly given the fact that both client and agency do not have exclusive relationships. The system of exploiting this is known as the 'ricochet.' Here is how it works. At the completion of the first genuinely cold canvass pitch, as part of the natural flow of small talk, marketing prospect A is asked the name of the ad agency planner with whom he or she works and whether that person might also be interested in the subject matter just presented. Usually both the information and go-ahead are given as a matter of course. This leads straight on to that target planner in agency B, who can hardly refuse a visit when the name of the client is quoted.

The prospection to B is clearly warm canvass and a much less daunting matter. Maintaining things at the warmer level continues by asking agency B which other marketing clients the planner services, and whether they could have an interest in the techniques discussed. Again no problems are envisaged and so an approach is made to that client, C, with a referral from the planner at B, which will ensure a positive reception. And this leads to another agency client D. So the ricochet continues, all now warm prospects. As a supplement to the cold canvass activities it provides the new business director with some 'lighter' relief. The case history at the end of this chapter provides a classic example of where the ricochet can lead, with the eventual sales success coming a long way from the initial input, but equally welcome whatever its source. Can it work for you?

This is how you work the ricochet –

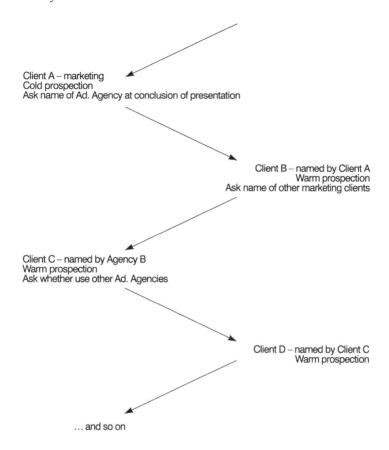

Client A – marketing
Cold prospection
Ask name of Ad. Agency at conclusion of presentation

Client B – named by Client A
Warm prospection
Ask name of other marketing clients

Client C – named by Agency B
Warm prospection
Ask whether use other Ad. Agencies

Client D – named by Client C
Warm prospection

... and so on

Finally, there is probably little need to remind you of the need to be constantly aware of other 'hit lists' that may be floating around your organization without the owner being aware of their potential value to you. In this context you should be thinking particularly of attendance lists from conferences/seminars/exhibitions that you and your own colleagues may have visited. These must be rescued from the dustbin and utilized. Don't hesitate to spend money on attendance at conferences and exhibitions yourself – just to gain the delegate list is worth the entrance fee.

If relevant to your business, think international. The technique about to be revealed will permit you to make appointments around the globe. With a combination of luck and careful planning you may be able to set up a sequence of meetings in nearby countries sufficient to enable a round trip to be organized, whereby the cost and time are sufficiently justified by a series of presentations to high potential prospects. I myself have managed this from a London base, organizing visits to Ireland, Switzerland and Belgium, all centres of concentration for multinationals, and offering major new business potential.

Each trip involved at least five presentations; the only risk being of last minute cancellations. Don't think that the prospective clients aren't flattered by such a visit. The same advice can apply to conferences and exhibitions, which are often set up on a regional scale.

2 Prospecting

You've got your (long) list of leads. Now you have to get in front of each of them in turn to be able to present your services. Prospecting, it's called. But how? By taking action yourself. Must I? Yes. Take courage, this will work! But only if you do it the right way.

This is the situation:

> 'I want Unigamble PLC as my client. I've done my homework, and qualified Natalie Smith as my lead, she is a new research director who is responsible for their major brand. She's the person I want to present my services to.'

So, what's your next step? Again, natural instincts must *not* be obeyed. The obvious approach is not necessarily the best approach. Nine times out of ten I have received from my audience the standard reply which goes as follows:

> 'Well, I'll send Natalie a letter introducing my company, enclosing our brochure, and asking permission to contact her a week or so later with the intention of making an appointment for me to visit her and go through our services in detail.'

Wrong! This will fail. When you call a week later, here is the reply you will get:

> 'Thank you for your letter. The enclosed brochure was very interesting and I've filed it away for reference when the need arises. So there is absolutely no need for you to visit me. I'll call you when I'm ready.'

Even if the above reply is true (and most likely it is simply a put-off; the brochure has been junked, the return call will never be made) you have not achieved your primary objective, your sole objective, which was to get face to face with your prospect. At this point in time it is your **only** objective, which is why this section is entitled prospecting and not selling. You are not even in a 'sales mode' right now. You have but one, simple goal and all your energies and efforts are devoted to that and no other: to make an appointment. And you have failed.

You will have failed because of both the manner and content of your approach. Manner: using the mail as first point of contact. Content: enclosing too much advance information of your services. **I want you to use the telephone**, not the mail (or even the fax, or e-mail). And I want you to severely restrict the amount of information you give at this stage.

Success depends on using the telephone and restricting your objective to the single focus of appointment getting. The telephone is **the** medium for prospecting, selling will be done in the face-to-face situation (and will be dealt with in the next chapter).

Only the telephone gives you the power, the impact and the immediacy swiftly and effectively to achieve your goal of getting that appointment. It allows you to be in control, hit your target off-guard, make your play and then quickly retire from the fray with most of your ammunition unused and ready to be applied in the eventual face-to-face situation.

To use the telephone effectively in this non-sales context requires application of a proven system: prospecting by telephone. If adopted it should enable you eventually to achieve appointments with at least 75 per cent of the targeted prospects you approach (over 90 per cent in cases of a genuinely unique service being offered to a willing audience).

The telephone as a medium has its deficiencies: it is impersonal, lacking warmth or eye contact and therefore making it difficult to judge responses. You cannot show anything, you cannot add colour – it is grey.

These should not concern you, since you are not in sales mode. You don't want to show anything yet; there is no need for human contact yet. All that awaits the meeting. To get to that meeting you need to make an appointment. For this purpose the telephone is king.

So back to the 3 Ps:

Prepare = homework and identification (Q × 2)

Prospect = attack – on the telephone

Present = sell – face to face

The benefits the telephone has to offer are much more relevant to you than its deficiencies in the appointment-getting prospecting mode:

efficiency and reach
the world of prospects (local, national, international) at your fingertips from your desk;
if successful you can fill your diary for a month after just a few days' calls

urgency
the most hassled prospect may drop everything he or she is doing to pick up the phone
when it rings

democracy
even the most senior prospect may drop everything he or she is doing to pick up the phone when you call – they don't know it's you; 'a pauper may speak to a king' – there is no limit to how high you can aim

predictability
you are calling; you initiate the opening exchange; reactions to it are predictable; so it . . .

... CAN BE SCRIPTED
in other words, you can be in control

Sitting at your desk, fully prepared, your homework done, a script in front of you (a script I will give you shortly) – you are now in a position to make a string of high level, high potential appointments literally within minutes. That's the power of the telephone.

But you need to learn how to use it. This may seem a crazy statement to make. You've used the telephone all your life. No lessons were or are necessary. Wrong. You've never used it this way before. You've never gambled all on hitting a target via the telephone and getting that target to do what you want. So you need instruction. You need help. And help comes in the form of a script.

It is possible that the word 'script' has made you wince. As an educated professional you react negatively to the idea of being straitjacketed by a set text. Note these wise words drawn from the autobiography of the world-renowned film and theatre director, Ingmar Bergman:

'Only he who is well prepared has any opportunity to improvise'

It is not my intention to cramp your style so long as you stay within the parameters and the fundamental philosophy that underlie the basic script. Until videophones become universal, no one will be able to see your script. You will adapt it to your needs so that you are fully comfortable with it. Eventually you will dispense with it since it will become second nature to you. Long before then you will not even sound like you are using a script. The script is your guide, but the words are yours to choose. The script is general, you will add the specifics. The script is a framework around which you will build your professional service offer. But not in any great detail, since you are aiming a bait at your prospect designed to achieve an appointment, not a sales pitch with full description of the offer.

Prospecting by telephone comprises four elements, which I will go on to describe in detail:

1 Planning
2 Script
3 Closing
4 Objections

Used wisely, adapted to your personality and your market, these steps will take you up to the threshold where your prospective clients work. It's not easy, there may be disappointment along the way, a few fish may escape, but in most cases you will be able to gain a sympathetic hearing for your services. A proportion will become your clients.

(1) Planning

Preparation, in the sense of basic homework, has already been discussed. You have your qualified leads – and lots of them. You know for each: their full name and designation; job title; areas of responsibility; their company's business sector – and, of course, their phone number. Now you are about to pick up the phone and go into live action.

Before doing so there are some small-scale personal/desktop preparations that are necessary and beneficial because they are confidence building. The personal items will arouse a wry smile, but are provided in good faith from those who have worked in the field for years. You are nervous – admit it. You anticipate rejection. I tell you, you will not be rejected – but you don't believe me. Well, at least there is one thing we can agree you don't want, and that's to be seen to fail, if it happens. So, make sure you have privacy; get an office where you are alone and where no one can hear or see you while you actually prospect. When you succeed, you'll whoop so loud they may be able to hear – but by then you won't care.

To get the adrenaline up and the motivation high you are recommended, as you dial, to adopt the three Ss:

Stand, Smile, Sing.

- **Stand:** to keep the muscles tense and alert; you can't be aggressive if you're slouched or with your feet up on the desk.
- **Smile:** to produce the correct, positive voice mood; a smile can be heard down the telephone, believe it.
- **Sing:** as you dial, to ensure a happy result! As you punch out those numbers, sing to yourself 'I'm gonna get you, I'm gonna get you' – anything to try and sound happy when in reality all you want to do is to cry, to escape this task!

Don't knock the three Ss; just use them!

Desktop preparations are more obvious. You should have within reach:

Your script
details follow; I call it 'your' script, because I want you to adapt my master text and own it

Diary/Calendar
calendar alongside diary, since long-term bookings may occur, and are not unwelcome

Two pens
*two pens, because one might fail and the whole process is so split-second you can afford
no lost moments as you search for an alternative*

Notepad
*because often the prospect will quite spontaneously provide valuable information which you
can utilize at the time of the visit*

Record sheet
*to monitor your own progress and log details such as when the prospect will be available if
not there when you first call*

You can see that our motto remains 'be prepared'. The whole process is fast and there is no room for mistakes. By being organized you can focus all your attention onto the task in hand. Another motto is 'predictability'. When the phone rings, you will know what is going to happen (details soon), but the prospect doesn't. The script ensures that you have the potential to remain in control until the call ends.

The script is dealt with below under the headings script/closing/objections. 'Script' is the basic text with its rationale; 'Closing' is getting the appointment; 'Objections' represent the problems you may meet (only rarely, believe me). You are strongly recommended to reproduce the entire text combining script and objections, keeping it in its entirety to one side of paper. Again, the purpose is for desktop speed and ease of reference when on the phone.

(2) The script

Your prospecting call will comprise these elements:

1 Greet, identify and ask a simple, factual 'Yes/No' question

Pause

2 Get prospect to speak/answer; immediately continue as planned
3 Gain interest – briefly, explain features and the personal benefit of your service offer
4 Establish best time to meet
5 Make appointment

Slow

6 Confirm appointment

Each of the elements has a clearly defined objective and a corresponding section in the script. Here first is the full text:

(SLOWLY) Good morning/afternoon, Mr/Mrs _____ My name is _____ and I'm director of _____; are you familiar with _____?

(PAUSE FOR RESPONSE)

Then, you'll know/Then, I can tell you – we are specialists in _____ and we've recently introduced a very interesting new service which allows you to _____ and that's why I'd like to come and tell you about it because I believe it could be of considerable value to you and your company. So would a _____ or a _____ suit you better, Mr/Mrs _____?

Fine, how would a _____ next week suit you? How about at _____ or perhaps a little later in the day?

Fine, so that's (SLOW) __ o'clock, on _____ day the _____ of this month.

Thank you very much, Mr/Mrs _____ I'll write to confirm that and I look forward to meeting you then.

Goodbye.

The underlying objectives are transparent but need emphasis and adherence. Element 1 is the salutation and identification of you and your company. Most crucial next step is the 'question' that links through to element 2. Even though it is hardly a demanding one, nor indeed is the nature of the actual answer of great import, the question's role is to gain a response. Any response! The need for this is that once the prospect has spoken there is a greatly reduced likelihood that he or she will later be able to reject you. Some contact, however tenuous, has been established with a result that the opportunity to be dismissive has diminished. In some ways you are no longer a stranger.

You must work hard to achieve a response from the prospect at the early stage. It is not easy. Your natural tendency will be to gabble away, determined to get your message across and reach your goal of closing with an appointment. Nerves will drive you on, the assumption being that as long as you are talking everything is still all right.

But it is not all right. You must pause, otherwise there is no real contact made, just a rapid monologue, and it will be quite easy for the listener to switch off and even slam down the phone on you without feeling they are being rude – rude to who? Just to a telephone gabbler?

Steel yourself to halt, get your response, confident in the knowledge that you can (regardless of the nature of the answer) move on again with your story. Which takes you to element 3. This is the nearest you will get to a sales pitch at this stage in the proceedings. You will have to present some aspect of your service now to gain interest – but it must be done in the most succinct manner possible. You have, in fact, to bait your trap in no more than a sentence or two in order to justify the appointment making that is your real objective. And personalize it – '. . . value to you . . .'. How you do this is entirely on your own judgement, with reference to your specific services, the client's needs (as assessed by you on the basis of your preparatory homework), and the ability to condense the offer into the time frame already mentioned. Remember to move from service feature to prospect benefit, even if the latter is simply a statement of how valuable your service will be . . . and to use the magic 'new' word always.

(3) Closing

Closing is an inherent part of the basic script, covering elements 4 to 6. But it deserves special attention because it is the objective of the whole exercise.

Remember not to start selling at the end of element 3; just arouse interest through your offer feature and its benefit and move straight on into the closing elements. Element 4 starts the closing routine, whereby you will find a suitable time and date, make the appointment (element 5) and then confirm it at element 6. The justification for the meeting is based on the interest established in your service, and that is your link to closing: 'in the light of this (valuable service)/that's why – I'd like to come and tell you about it . . .'

A crucial feature of the latter stages is to leave the prospect with a 'yes . . . yes' decision rather than 'yes . . . no'. It entails suggesting alternative meeting options and focusing the attention on the choice between them rather than allowing a choice between **a** meeting and **no** meeting. In other words, not 'do you want to see me?' but rather 'when shall we meet?' expressed as ' . . . so would a . . . or a . . . suit you better?' filling in the blanks with something like 'mornings or afternoons' or 'earlier or later in the week'.

You must get something into the diary at this stage, however far ahead. There is genuinely no limit to the future time scale you should be prepared to accept. Because one thing is clear; once your name has been entered into the diary it will never be removed. A commitment has been made by the prospect that will not be retracted (even though postponements are routine and will have to be accepted with good grace, cancellations are rare).

Before moving on to dealing with possible objections, let's consider some classical prospection scripts that you may wish to use. These cover elements 1 to 6, and in the majority of cases they alone will be sufficient to get you to your appointment. The scripts follow the principles I have explained, but are not rigid and you will see how they allow for personal and profession-specific adaptations, both in the general wording and, in particular, the specific 'bait' you will use to excite interest. And remember, objections are not the norm – things CAN go as smoothly as this.

> 'Good morning John, my name is Michael Roe and I'm V-P of Research International, Europe's leading market research agency. Have you had dealings with us before John . . . Well, that's why I'm contacting you. We've just launched a new system which allows you to measure the brand equity of your own and competitive brands, providing you with a simple index number, something which is certain to be of considerable

value to you and your company, and that's why I would like to meet you to tell you about it – so would a morning or afternoon be better for you . . . Fine, so we'll make it a morning during the week of the Xrd, shall we say the Yrd at 11.00 . . . Good, so that's fixed. Thank you. Goodbye.'

'Good afternoon, Sheila. This is Richard Friend calling, I'm MD of the exhibitions organization World Trade Fairs. Have you come across our name before, Sheila . . . Great, then you'll know that we have always offered the very best in stand design, but we now have a unique multimedia integration stand which could meet all your company's interactive needs, and that's what I would like to come and show you – so which day would suit you best in the coming weeks . . . Yes, I could do a date next month if your diary before that is full, how about the Yth . . . Fine, let's go for that, at 2.30. Thank you. Goodbye.'

'Good morning, Mr Marcus. My name is Pollack, and I'm the senior partner and S, N and P Legal, where I head up the Copyright Protection team. Are you aware off our services . . . Well, I'm not surprised Mr Marcus. But it really is a shame that our success in this sector is not better known because I do believe we could be of tremendous assistance to you and your organization with our new Internet Forgery Searchengine, which offers you an itemized service. That's what I would like to explain to you at a meeting, and I wondered if early or later in the week generally suits you better . . . Right, we'll make it a Monday then – the Xrd, at 11.00? OK. Thank you. Goodbye.'

'Is that Barry Lester? Hello, Mr Lester, this is Ian Wright, senior partner of Streets, Quantity Surveyors. Am I right in thinking that you have just taken up a European responsibility in your organization . . . Oh, that's good, congratulations. That makes what I want to tell you about very relevant. One thing you may not already know is that we have just linked up with Bau A.G. and so are now represented all over Europe, where we could meet your multinational needs, and that's what I'd like to expand on in a meeting with you, when I can show you our existing services and precisely where we operate – so would a date early or late next month be more convenient for you . . . Yes, around the 10th would be good for me too. Shall we say the 11th at 3.00? Thank you. Goodbye.'

These are conversations – they lead to appointments. The words of the prospects are not recorded, but they do exist; these are not monologues. The responses are not relevant *per se*, they will vary in each case; the prospects are being carried along on your agenda to your objective.

For the purposes of instruction only, let's just consider one or two bad scripts – so that you know what to avoid. They are bad because they do not follow the rules – they permit no response from the prospect, or offer a rejection possibility, or show uncertainty/lack of confidence/no belief in yourself or your service, or, finally, offer no real reason to meet, no benefit for the prospect to take out of such a meeting – so why should an appointment be granted?

> 'Good morning, Mr Smith. I hope you're not too busy. Have you got a moment? I am calling from Rhino Design, and we can help you get those brochures done. I know you've probably got a supplier already, but I wonder if I could come and show you what we can do?'

NO, you can't!

> 'Hello there, I'm calling from D, D and Y and we can provide an answer to all your PR needs, when would it be convenient for me to call round and show you what we can do – I'm in your area next Thursday seeing a few other people?'

Well, lucky old you; waste their time then, not mine!

Let's quickly get back to the successful approaches. Now that you have your appointment you can at last revert to your natural impulse to go into print by offering to mail a written confirmation of the appointment. But not until you are sure the prospect has noted it down in his or her diary, and only as reassurance and for transparency (offering a chance to see both your and your company's names in print).

The written confirmation should abide by the rules already set – it should be sent off immediately, be brief, and not attempt to do the sales job. So don't enclose any brochure or sales material. Simply confirm the appointment in an unambiguous way, without apologies or reservations.

Here is a classic example –

COMPANY LETTERHEAD

Dear Mr Marcus,

Just a brief note to confirm the appointment we made during yesterday's telephone conversation. I shall call on you at your offices on Monday 17th April 1999 at 11.00 a.m. to present my company's Internet Forgery Searchengine.

I look forward to meeting you then,

Yours sincerely,

Martin Pollack
Senior Partner

(4) Objections

Your mind is going to be dominated by thoughts of these objections. You will have considered my proposed script good but idealistic. In the real world you know it will never happen like that: 'I'll be ignored, ridiculed, abused, shouted at, and in every conceivable way made to regret I ever had the cheek to think I could sell.' This is the source of your fear of even starting on the process.

A sea change is required in your thinking on this topic, and it will be achieved here. Begin by reminding yourself of the value of your services and the need for the prospect to be informed of what is available on the market. Then remember you are a professional talking, not selling, to an equal. **So why should there be any objection at all to the meeting you are attempting to arrange?**

In the majority of cases your approach will be accepted without argument. Using the above script you will find yourself closing on the appointment and with your phone back in its cradle within in a minute of having begun your pitch! That's the reality.

But you still don't believe it; and you do need to be prepared for the occasional genuine objection/difficult situation. Once again a technique exists to enable you to win through. It is based on the following premises:

1 objections are predictable;
2 they are hurdles not brick walls;
3 often they are just a mirage;
4 they represent real human 'contact' with the prospect.

Consider then what objections to your visit could indeed be raised. How many can you yourself come up with? The prospect will produce no others. It is unlikely that there will be more than the nine listed below (the italics underneath are designed to remove the immediate sting; the following pages show you how to react and continue towards your objective):

1 Happy with/Using competition
   Not exactly a surprise, so no need for this to knock you off course
2 Too expensive
   Maybe, but are we comparing like with like? Prices are project based and not rate-card. What about value?
3 Used you before and found you unsatisfactory
   This is serious indeed, but the 'you' was the company not 'you' personally and we know that people buy people – so there remains hope of recovery
4 Not in the market at present/No budget left
   Irrelevant to you – you're in for the long term, not for an immediate sale
5 You're too big and sophisticated; we're small
   OK flatter them with your attention
6 Tell me more now/Put something in the post
   Danger, danger, danger!

7 Too busy
  Again, hardly a surprising excuse nowadays – so don't be distracted from your purpose
8 Not interested
  Isn't it necessary to be alert to what's on the market? Since when was ignorance bliss?
9 I'll think about it
  Let me help the thought process

Since you can foresee all these objections, the corollary is that you can prepare to meet and overcome them. On the rare occasions when they are raised you will then be able to respond immediately. And the technique you will use will involve:

1 acceptance of the objection;
2 neutralization of it;
3 presentation of an alternative view;
4 returning to your original script and aiming at the close.

In every case shown above the script that follows insists that, rather like a boxer, you ride with the punch, don't argue with the prospect, reassure them with a new proposition, and then return, single-mindedly to your one and only objective of getting that appointment. So even should you be faced with an unanticipated objection the same principles should be applied and lead to ultimate success. Remember to have this script in front of you, so you will be prepared – you are working to a well-constructed plan while your prospect is ad libbing.

The full script for achieving your goal is shown following. After each reply you can assume that the script always comes back to the '... so would ...' line attempting to set up the meeting – '... so would a morning or afternoon be better for you?' or similar.

Closing with an appointment is the only thing on your mind; preventing it is not dominant in your prospect's mind. The odds are in your favour – you have a greater sense of purpose than your target at this stage – and you should be able to attain your goal.

| Happy with/Using competition | Fine. They're a good company, I know of them. I'd simply like to meet you to show you our new services, so that in future you'll have a broader choice of/be in a better position to evaluate between agencies ... so would ...
OR
Fine. They're a good company, I know of them. But I'm sure you'll agree that in such a fast-moving business as ours, it is always valuable to be up to date with what is on offer, and that's why I would like to meet you ... so would ... |

Too expensive	I take your point Mr/Ms ... but there have been some changes recently in our pricing structure and I think when we meet you'll appreciate how cost competitive our services now are ... so would ...
Used before and found unsatisfactory	I'm sorry to hear that Mr ... but I believe our new services like ... would be of great interest to you. They've been very successful for others in your sector and that's why I'd like to come and show you how ... so would ...
Not in the market at present/No budget left	I appreciate that Mr ..., it would have been fortunate indeed if I'd phoned just when you were on the point of commissioning. But there are several new aspects of our service which I believe could be of benefit to you in the future, and that's what I'd like to tell you about when we meet ... so would ...
You're too big and sophisticated; we're small	I hear what you say Mr ..., but I suggest that a meeting would enable us to work out how we could tailor our new service to fit your particular requirements ... so would ...
Tell me more now/ Put something in the post	As you can imagine Mr ... our services are customized so I would need to know more of your particular needs and that can best be done when we meet ... so would ...
Too busy	I understand that Mr ... that's why I'm telephoning for an appointment some time ahead. Let's fix a time for when you're less busy ... so would ...
Not interested	I wouldn't expect you to be interested in something new that you haven't had a chance of learning about. I'll have a chance to put that right when we meet ... so would ...
I'll think about it	Certainly Mr ..., but do remember you're under no obligation, so I think you'll be in the best position to make up your mind after we meet ... so would ...

A few additional notes regarding each of the main objections may be of value. Going down the list:

● Don't denigrate the competition, particularly if your prospect is using them already. By doing so, you are actually denigrating the prospect, since he or she has selected them and you are implying that that decision was wrong. Admit to the strengths of the rival, but simply offer your own as being unique and/or complementary.
● Professional services are unlikely to be rate-card based, so you can always escape criticism of previous pricings by referring to your project-based pricing structure or a new price policy.
● Professional services are people businesses, and so a previous bad experience can be blamed on an individual and not taken as a general indictment.

- Not being in the market at present is easy to overcome – you are offering information for future use, not instant sales.
- Size is no barrier – professional services are inherently flexible in sophistication.
- Resisting the request to 'put a brochure in the post' is not easy. But it must be resisted, for the reason already given – it is guaranteed to result in your failure to get that appointment. This may involve a small white lie, of the 'out of print' type. Even better is to stress the true fact that professional services are customized and so a brochure cannot be tailored to individual needs.
- The 'too busy' excuse may be mitigated by the offer to phone you back. It is often the case that a secretary or assistant will offer to take your name and number and get the prospect to call you. Do not accept. For two reasons: first, nine times out of ten they will not call you back (it's just an excuse); second, if they do call, you are immediately at a disadvantage, being caught unawares, possibly without your script at hand and therefore not in control.

3 Further elements of prospecting

It has never been my intention to underplay the difficulty of getting started on the prospecting road. There is in reality only one single event that can remove the fear and turn pain into pleasure: success in achieving an appointment. Then there will be no stopping you and you will want to go on all day. (Sadly, however, coming in to the office the next day will put you back to square one, the nerves returning in full measure; it seems the adrenaline is not long lasting.)

Here are some twelve further tips, in no particular order, that may help you surmount the daily hurdle.

I Telephone rules of speech

Always bear in mind that you are using the telephone and that it has its strengths and weaknesses. Remember the following features:

- *Speak slowly*: probably the most difficult of the rules of speech to observe. This is as a result of nerves and only constant practice and actual success will gradually slow you down. A machine-gun gabble is disastrous, for its own sake and because it will almost certainly result in you missing the strategic, scripted pause. At the top of my own script I always write in bold capitals – **SLOW – SLOW – SLOW**.
- *Enthuse*: just as I stated earlier that a smile can be transmitted down the phone-line, so enthusiasm is infectious and smoothes the acceptance process.
- *Be expressive*: avoid a monotone.
- *Pause strategically*: as indicated in the script.
- *Enunciate clearly*.
- *Don't interrupt*: apart from the fact that it is rude, it is most likely that if the prospect wants to say something it will probably be a positive and useful item, rather than abuse.

2 Timing (x 2)

1 You want to catch your prospects at their desks, in a receptive mood, without any secretarial or voicemail (see below) barriers. Obviously the best times to achieve such a result are at the beginning and end of the day, i.e. between 8.00 and 9.30 a.m. or after 5.30 p.m. Not only are these the most productive periods for you, but they also create an impression of one hard-working professional getting in touch with another. There is no general agreement about the best days of the week to utilize. Some claim that Mondays and Fridays are not ideal, especially Monday mornings and Friday evenings. I disagree. My own experience is that these days work well. At such moments, prospects are indeed concerned with other matters, but that very pressure makes them want to get rid of you quickly – and since the general rule is that they are not rude, the easiest and quickest route 'out' for them is to give you what you want, which is the appointment, because then you will also be happy to get off the phone quickly. Certainly, I would advise that you avoid the central section of the working day, not because prospects will be less amenable then, but simply because so many will be unobtainable – stuck in meetings, or out of their offices. This advice fits in with the general philosophy of my book – namely that these techniques are to be adopted by you but are only a part of your function. So, use the start and close of the day for prospection; for the remainder of the day, continue in your professional role.

2 Be honest in your reply if the prospect asks you how long the visit will take – no 'white lies' or being economical with the truth.

3 Have your entire script on ONE page in front of you

(SLOWLY) Good morning/afternoon, Mr/Mrs ＿＿＿＿＿＿ My name is
＿＿＿＿＿＿ and I'm director of ＿＿＿＿＿＿; are you familiar with
＿＿＿＿＿＿ ?

(PAUSE FOR RESPONSE)

Then, you'll know/Then, I can tell you – we are specialists in ＿＿＿＿＿＿
and we've recently introduced a very interesting new service which allows you to
＿＿＿＿＿＿ and that's why I'd like to come and tell you about it because I believe
it could be of considerable value to you and your company. So would a ＿＿＿＿＿＿
or ＿＿＿＿＿＿ suit you better?

Fine, how would a ＿＿＿＿＿＿ next week suit you? How about at ＿＿＿＿＿＿
or perhaps a little later in the day?

Fine, so that's (SLOW) ＿ o'clock, on ＿＿＿＿ day the ＿＿＿＿ of this month.

Thank you very much, Mr/Mrs ＿＿＿＿＿＿ I'll write to confirm that and I look
forward to meeting you then.

Goodbye.

Happy with/Using competition	Fine. They're a good company, I know of them. I'd simply like to meet you to show you our new services, so that in future you'll have a broader choice of/be in a better position to evaluate between agencies ... so would ... OR Fine. They're a good company, I know of them. But I'm sure you'll agree that in such a fast-moving business as ours, it is always valuable to be up to date with what is on offer, and that's why I would like to meet you ... so would ...
Too expensive	I take your point Mr/Ms ... but there have been some changes recently in our pricing structure and I think when we meet you'll appreciate how cost competitive our services now are ... so would ...
Used before and found unsatisfactory	I'm sorry to hear that Mr ... but I believe our new services like ... would be of great interest to you. They've been very successful for others in your sector and that's why I'd like to come and show you how ... so would ...
Not in the market at present/No budget left	I appreciate that Mr ..., it would have been fortunate indeed if I'd phoned just when you were on the point of commissioning. But there are several new aspects of our service which I believe could be of benefit to you in the future, and that's what I'd like to tell you about when we meet ... so would ...
You're too big and sophisticated; we're small	I hear what you say Mr ..., but I suggest that a meeting would enable us to work out how we could tailor our new service to fit your particular requirements ... so would ...
Tell me more now/Put something in the post	As you can imagine Mr ... our services are customized so I would need to know more of your particular needs and that can best be done when we meet ... so would ...
Too busy	I understand that Mr ... that's why I'm telephoning for an appointment some time ahead. Let's fix a time for when you're less busy ... so would ...
Not interested	I wouldn't expect you to be interested in something new that you haven't had a chance of learning about. I'll have a chance to put that right when we meet ... so would ...
I'll think about it	Certainly Mr ..., but do remember you're under no obligation, so I think you'll be in the best position to make up your mind after we meet ... so would ...

4 The secretary

A good secretary can undoubtedly act as an almost impenetrable barrier between you and your prospect. Hence the advice, in point 2 above, for you to try to avoid her (sorry to be sexist) by phoning at the times of day when she is less likely to be present. But it should be remembered that a growing number of even quite senior personnel no longer have secretarial assistance. Coping with voicemail is now an issue of equal relevance (and dealt with in point 6 below).

Only limited advice can be given for coping with a good secretary, because a good secretary is insurmountable. The good news is that there are very few good secretaries. So the advice below may well work in many of the limited number of cases where you come across a secretary. The objections that secretaries raise are basically no different from those already detailed – the most common being those of 'write a letter' or 'send a brochure' to the boss. You must not do so, attempting to deal with this objection in the manner already prescribed.

In general:

- Determine whether the secretary herself keeps the prospect's diary and, if so, employ the prospection skills described here to achieve an appointment diary entry via her. She is to all intents and purposes now your prospect and can be approached as such.
- Push to speak to the prospect directly, i.e. simply demand, without being rude but certainly by being insistent through your manner and tone of voice (maybe use an inflated job title for yourself to show that she is not dealing with your common or garden salesperson but a senior professional, someone whose status at least matches that of her boss).
- Get and use a referral as a battering ram. The trickle down from a senior in the company will work most effectively here. There can be a temptation to tell a white lie, i.e. to use the superior's or outsider's name even if you haven't actually spoken to them – resist it. I've said earlier that you can and should aim high, so do it and get lucky or get passed on, in which case the referral is real and you will feel justified in using it.
- Get your secretary to call the prospect's secretary, hoping that the 'freemasonry' of secretaries will do the trick. Accept any denigration of your character that may be required from your secretary in order to further this aim – your helplessness, your job being on the line – whatever she needs to gain the sympathy of her opposite number!
- Finally, and more in hope than expectation, the following has been known to be effective – blind the secretary with science. It works like this: 'I'd like to speak to Mr/Mrs ... regarding the use of *multifactorialmicroprocessingtextual* services!' Pause. Hopefully she will be at a loss as to how to respond and it now becomes an easier option for her to put you through than to resist or admit to her own ignorance. (The gobbledegook phrase may be real or a white lie.)

5 Log your results

Using a record sheet has already been referred to. But think of using it not just to record the vital call results but also to register your own judgement on your performance. Do this and keep trying to improve. Before each new day review your assessment of the previous day's performance. Keep practising.

In this context my strong advice is never to start on a period of cold calling without a sizeable batch of prospect leads in your hand. It is certain that your first few calls will be stymied by prospects being in meetings, on holiday, sick, etc. and it is all too easy to run through ten or more leads without ever having had the opportunity even to practise your script. Since you will have taken time and trouble to get your mental state and personal organization all set for the big event, it is very wasteful to have to call a halt in order to generate new leads. It is recommended that you have at least twenty available before you start, and to put aside a whole morning for cold canvass.

A sample record sheet is shown on page 65. Keep one for each prospect. Adapt it to your own needs.

Remember, it is a numbers game. You will have to make hundreds of calls as the weeks and months go by, eventually thousands, to get to enough targets. That's no problem thanks to the speed and efficiency of the telephone. So what results can you expect at the first call you make to each lead?

1 No direct contact – busy, blocked, absent, travelling, holiday, etc.
   fact of life; record and move details to next day's hit list
2 Appointment – no objection
   success
3 Appointment – after objection raised
   success, but you had to work for it
4 Prospect wants special letter
   you shouldn't have allowed this to happen – success is now unlikely
5 Secretarial/voicemail block
   too bad – you tried
6 No chance
   you were blown out; don't pine, move on to the next

Generally speaking the rates associated with each of these AT THE FIRST CALL are (go ahead and record your own):

1	57%
2	10%
3	10%
4	3%
5	8%
6	12%

Record Sheet – Prospection

Prospect name   _____

Designation   _____

Title   _____

Company   _____

Phone no.   _____

Fax no.   _____

NOTES

Contact attempts	Date/Time	Reason – if no contact	Self assessment
1			
2			
3			
4			
5			
APPOINTMENT	_____ _____		

NOTES FOR MEETING
map/issues/materials/etc.

Another reason to start with a multitude of leads is to catch the wind of success when it occurs. To give yourself the best chance of this you need to work with large numbers. Result 2 or 3 – an appointment fixed – is the best incentive to continue there can be; so have the leads available to keep chasing until you hit your first target of the day.

6 Overcoming voicemail

The modern scourge, and continuing to grow! There is as yet no 'industry standard' answer to this problem. Choosing the right time to call, when voicemail might not be switched on, is always an objective. But meeting voicemail head on and beating it is not so easy. Certainly, the *'hello Mr X, my name is Y and I would like to talk to you about ZZZ; please give me a call on 12345'* is likely to have only limited effect, and to be no use at all if it is spoken at nervous speed with the vital call-back number incomprehensible – who the hell would take the trouble to put effort into calling back an unknown and obvious salesperson?

Here is a possible solution, not fully validated but recommended for trial. The philosophy behind it is counter-intuitive and so of interest; maybe you could adapt it yourself! The concept is to fully use the free time afforded by the voicemail machine and direct a slow, clear and emphatic monologue at it – sticking to the script principle (now with no one to interrupt you!). Since by definition you cannot close in this situation, you have instead to 'threaten' to call back again at a specific time on a specific date to attain your objective of achieving an appointment – and you need to carry out that threat.

When the voicemail beep sounds, you deliver your script in a clear and steady voice, concluding with, first, a careful and repeated enunciation of your name and contact number, and, second, the statement that if you do not hear from the target by a specific date you will call again (not a threat but a promise!). When you do call again, as it is certain you will have to, you start by referring to the promise made last time and then go through the script, again finishing with the renewed promise of a further call. And do it! As this saga continues the tone should become chattier, even joking about the nature of your persistence (emphasizing the target's importance to you) and dropping in snippets of personal news that may have occurred in the meantime – in other words a 'virtual' relationship is being built up rather than an aggressive hunt. Chances are, you will be contacted after the fourth or fifth time you have yourself called, the target realizing that he or she cannot escape your persistence, and yet feeling somewhat flattered and personally 'involved' with you. Don't be caught out yourself – keep the names of these targets firmly in front of your eyes on your desk or wall so that you can immediately respond to the contact with your virtual 'friend'.

7 Who are you?

A strange question maybe, but of some importance.

> 'Good morning, Mr Smith. This is Michael Roe speaking, and I'm
> new business development director for Research International ...'

Not a serious problem, but doesn't it give the game away, putting the emphasis on selling and removing the 'professional to professional' status that underlies this book? The same might apply if you designated yourself as marketing manager or sales director.

In my opinion a white lie is acceptable here. Be who you want to be, but best of all, be who your prospect would like you to be. Pander to snobbery if necessary at this stage at least. I would suggest you avoid the titles named above and keep to research director, senior partner, executive director, V-P Consultancy Services, etc.

Can you over-egg it, i.e. go in too high – CEO, chairman? In my opinion, not. They will be flattered.

8 Filling your diary

What can be pleasanter than seeing your diary gradually fill with cold canvass visits? Beware – your appointment is rated 'lowest of the low' in your prospect's diary, highly susceptible to being pushed out for more pressing engagements. And not unfairly so. It is not the top priority. You will just have to live with postponements, which often means that what appears to be a full week as you look ahead, later becomes full of gaps. My message is to fill your diary slightly beyond what you regard as ideal in the knowledge that it will thin out as the date approaches (but don't double book, that would be too risky!).

It is also very important to remember that while postponements are common, cancellations are rare. In fact you must resist them tooth and nail. When the call comes through requesting your appointment be changed: (1) you must not be despondent and assume rejection; rather accept it as a fact of life and go ahead and re-book; (2) you must not allow it to become a cancellation; get back to your objections list – all we have here is another form of objection which needs to be overcome (and it's easy; after all, the prospect made an appointment and does not really want to admit to changing his or her mind or to having been coerced – so use the trusted technique to get back to 'which *other* morning or afternoon would suit you better?').

9 Be prepared for pleasant surprises

Your nervousness, anticipation of rejection, and insecurity have a tendency to blind you to the potential for good news. In other words you may be so busy working your script, making apologies for presumed disturbance, etc., that you do not hear or detect the prospect expressing genuine interest, possibly slightly at a tangent to your main thrust. You must make sure that you do not miss this, that you maintain your alertness (your antennae) so as to be able to take it on board, show flexibility and allow yourself to divert from script so as to grasp the unexpected chance that is being held out to you and therefore is well within your reach. So always keep listening!

As an example, I have found myself in full flow when the slow realization dawns that my prospect is not only requiring no further convincing from me, but is actually already presenting a problem for solution in the expectation that I am a suitable supplier. I was being briefed before I had even achieved the appointment; in fact the appointment may even be unnecessary – the prospect would probably already be a client by then!

'Serendipity' is the relevant word – a happy confluence of chance events which allows you your breakthrough. The prospect may have just blown out his current supplier due to a poor performance; may have only yesterday received orders from his senior to find a consultant for an unusual project; may be wrestling with an intractable problem where you have specific expertise to offer; may have lost a member of staff to maternity leave and urgently requires to outsource, etc. Your call at this particular time becomes providential and so is successful. You call it luck. But, in fact, you have made your own luck.

10 Don't worry about personnel changes

> 'He's left the company'

> 'She's on maternity leave'

These are not responses to dread. Most likely each implies one prospect has become two. In the first case, the staff change, chase the original incumbent, who is more than likely to be in as equally interesting a position for your services as he or she was before (probably more so, as most moves are for promotion); then attack the new appointee as you had originally planned. In the second case, the maternity replacement, however temporary, is a target who may move on to another responsible position when the new mother returns, so go ahead with your pitch as planned.

11 Allow yourself no excuses

Put a planned part of the day aside in your diary for prospection. Then accept no excuses to avoid the task – and believe me you will think of many! Prospection will become a mountain that you will try anything to avoid. Nerves will be on edge. There will be any number of more attractive options. They are just distractions. Force yourself.

Don't even attempt to cold canvass from open-plan offices. Indeed should you wish to follow all the advice given here (remember the three Ss!) you will be well advised to shut yourself away where no one can see you.

12 Ride out disappointment

OK I admit it – sometimes you will fail to get your target. This has been the unspoken agenda all along. I have talked of high success rates, of appointments made, of secretaries overcome, of possible contact at the highest level which succeeds, even if you get passed down the line . . . and so on. All this ignores the possibility of failure. So let's bring it out into the open, however briefly.

IF – you are faced with rudeness, move right on to the next on your list and put it out of your mind (it is rare, you were unlucky).

IF – you are faced with outright rejection, accept it and move on to the next prospect there and then, without pause for reflection or despondency and never failing to analyse your own performance to check whether the task was truly impossible.

IF – you are beaten by a secretary or voicemail, just remember you are in good company.

BUT – often failure is your own fault, and I don't just mean lack of proper application of the techniques described. Planning may let you down – my own worst moments have been getting a response such as 'Don't you know I'm already working with X in your organization?' or 'But Y in your company called me only last week – don't you guys talk to each other?'

Right . . . now we've confessed to the downside – it is clear your success remains mostly in your own hands . . . so just do it!

. . . and do it again, and again. Keep practising. When your first call has just finished, you cradle the receiver, the sweat is on your forehead, and you realize you made a mess of it (probably gabbling like a machine-gun) – don't despair. Why should you have been perfect first time? Record your self-assessment, and pick up the phone immediately again. (It might, however, be worthwhile to have anticipated this early difficulty, and not have selected the most attractive prospect from your list to practise on!)

ALARM! EMERGENCY!

You're thinking – 'No, sorry, it still scares the pants off me. Can't I subcontract this task to a bureau?' My answer is in principle 'no', in practice it is possible. Theoretically, how can an outsider make the impression required and not be found out to be an impostor, even on such a quick-fire contact as the prospecting call? It cannot work, except by being economical with the truth should the prospect press for answers to questions such as 'who exactly are you?' Are you really willing to put your company's reputation into the front line with major prospects using an outsider? Shouldn't you rise to the challenge yourself, using the skills imparted by this book, set a fine example to your company and colleagues, and reap the rewards yourself of the guaranteed success that we promise?

Well yes, but the fear factor is sometimes irresistible, and if a specialist consultancy comes and offers to take the matter off your hands, why not accept? I know of those that have been satisfied, so I cannot deny that it is possible. Since there are now many such agencies available, all that can be said is vet them carefully before you entrust them with the task of representing you in such a high profile way.

Demand to see the script and have total control over the hit list of prospects. Discuss very carefully with them how they will present themselves – will they be acting 'on behalf' of the company or 'as a member' of your company? If the latter, what will they give out as contact number should the prospect need to communicate? Make sure they understand the minimal basics of your professional service and any technique they may feature in their script. Attend some call sessions as an observer and insist that only the seniors who you have met actually make the calls. Agree on what basis payment will be made – per effective appointment should be the terms, rather than attempts made.

The fact that it is possible for such agencies to work successfully confirms the philosophy of this chapter – that the prospection call is a skill independent of the service being canvassed, and that there is no need (indeed, no possibility for such agencies) to enter into details – 'get in and get out without questions' is the only way they can function.

A cautionary tale

(courtesy of Barry Marcus)

A few times in the preceding text the words 'white lie' have appeared. This would appear dissonant with the 'professional' tone underlying the skills being promoted in the book. In prospection there is often the temptation to allow the end to justify the means; who will remember or even notice a small white lie on the way to greater things? Here is a warning.

> As the little old lady entered his small shop the butcher groaned inwardly, preparing to deal with his most fussy and difficult customer.
>
> 'I'll have a chicken today', she said, and in response he pulled out a trussed fowl for her inspection.
>
> She pinched and prodded the bird all over, giving it her usual thorough inspection while the butcher stood patiently by, rage building up.
>
> 'No', she stated, 'I'm not fully satisfied with this one. Show me another.'
>
> Taking back the original and placing it under the counter, the butcher realized that he had no other chickens that day. An evil

thought entered his mind – here was an opportunity for a little revenge on his tormentor.

Placing the same chicken back on the counter, he said 'Here you are, madam, I'm sure you'll find this far better.'

Again the little old lady went through her rigorous inspection routine, and the butcher's face almost broke into a huge grin as he heard her say 'Yes, that's much better, I'll take that one.'

Full of satisfaction, the butcher began to wrap the chicken when he heard her continue:

'I tell you what, you've been so kind, I think I'll take them both!'

Sample prospections

All along my purpose has been to convince you of the need to make appointments and to provide you with a model of the process itself, so that you may gain the motivation and the reassurance to prospect for yourself. What more can I offer? Well I could go beyond exhortation and move to example – prospection in action. Why not provide some samples of the types of telephone prospection calls that can really happen to show how successful they can be, whether the prospect is amenable or hesitant or even resistant (and, believe me, most will be amenable)? So here are five scenarios of varying difficulty. Once again, all are from my own field of market research – names have been changed to protect the innocent. Just substitute your own professional service prospect/ offer as you read them. You might also like to note how brief the whole telephonic prospection process is, even in cases where there are objections. Any 'harshness' you might perceive in the process will soon be forgotten by the recipient as he or she gets on with the hassle of everyday life in the office after your call; it will certainly disappear before the date of the appointment. It is further mitigated by the fact that the telephone has been the contact mode, there has been no face-to-face interaction, which means the 'proximity' factor is reduced and any residual 'bruising' will soon be soothed by your own friendly and helpful demeanour when you both meet – I hope!

I Miss Nice

Prospect – Natalie Smith, director of research, Unigamble plc

Background – Unigamble regularly launch new household cleaning products aimed at housewives

Assumed need – to gain advance information on the likely sales success of new brands they may consider launching

Benefit – my company has a technique that predicts sales volume potential before market launch

ME: Good morning, Natalie. My name is Michael Roe, and I'm an executive director at the market research agency called Research International. Tell me, Natalie, have you heard of Research International?

NATALIE: Er, no I don't think I've come across your company . . .

ME: Well, actually we are the country's largest ad hoc research agency, and our main specialism is in the area of new product development research. Our MicroTest technique forecasts the potential sales volume of new products at an early stage in their development, which means you get a sales estimate, and I think this could be of great value to you and your company and that's why I'd like to come and explain it to you – so, Natalie, are mornings or afternoon generally better for you?

NATALIE: It does sound interesting, does it provide a conversion ratio between trial and adoption over various distribution cycles and . . .

ME: That's exactly what I'll explain when we meet, so would a week early or later next month be better? I've got my diary open at the week of the 9th – looking at Tuesday the 10th in the morning . . .?

NATALIE: Yes, mornings are generally better, but could we rather make it on the Wednesday?

ME: That's OK – so I'm noting down in my diary . . . that I come to your offices on . . . Wednesday the 11th . . . at, shall we say, 10 o'clock?

NATALIE: How long will we need?

ME: I think about forty-five minutes should be sufficient.

NATALIE: All right.

ME: What I'll do, Natalie, is write you a brief note this week confirming this appointment, and on it you'll have my address and phone and fax numbers if you need to contact me beforehand. My name is Michael Roe, that's spelt R – O – E, from Research International. I look forward to meeting you on the 17th. Thank you . . . goodbye!

Commentary – too good to be true? No, this style of conversation is the norm, not the exception. The prospect has the need, I have the answer – why should she refuse to see me? My product works (it was designed for just such a client) so I may be able to make her job easier – let's get together. The description given of the product was only brief, and I was not drawn into a detailed discussion on the phone, but it was sufficient to arouse interest and clearly indicate the benefit to the prospect. The remainder of the conversation flow was almost as scripted. The difficulty in knowing the precise marital status of women, and hence whether they prefer Miss, Mrs or Ms, drives me to take the risk right at the outset of using her Christian name. (I could have called the switchboard in advance and asked how she likes to be addressed – but they don't always know.) I was honest about the time required when we meet – if I had said 'only ten minutes' in the expectation of her being more amenable to a short appointment, it would simply have destroyed the credibility and importance of my offer! The confirmatory letter is both for her reassurance and my own maintenance of pressure – it says 'yes, the conversation actually happened and you made a commitment'.

2 Mr Difficult

Prospect – Stephen White, marketing director, Bank Direct
Background – a new telephone banking service
Assumed need – to monitor customer satisfaction
Benefit – my company has a new technique that does more than just measure customer satisfaction – it diagnoses the strengths and weaknesses

ME: Good afternoon Mr White, my name is Michael Roe and I'm executive director at the market research agency Research International – are you familiar with Research International Mr White?

STEVE: Of course I am, I've even used you some years ago when I was with Midscot Bank.

ME: Well that's good, Steve, but you may not be familiar with our more recently developed customer service measurement technique called SMART which provides you with those importance values you need for each service attribute, so allowing you to prioritize them. I think this could be of great value to you and your bank and I'd like to come and tell you about it – are mornings or afternoons generally better for you?

STEVE: I'm using the TNA Agency for my customer satisfaction work nowadays, and I'm very happy with what they do, so I think I'll pass on that, thank you.

ME: Yes, they're a good agency, we have a lot of respect for them, but I think you'll find our SMART technique offers some extra, unique benefits for you and your bank – which is why I'd like to come and tell you about it – I wonder, would a morning or afternoon suit you better in the coming weeks?

STEVE: I think it'll be much too heavyweight and expensive for us

ME: Well, you're right it's certainly not cheap, but I think you'll find that the extra analyses it provides make for real value, and that's what I'd like to show you when we meet – I've my diary open on a morning next week . . .?

STEVE: I'm really not sure that it'll be of interest to me, and it'll just be a waste of your time.

ME: Of course, I understand that you can't be sure right now because I haven't given you all the details about it, so you'd be in a better position to judge after a meeting, and I'm happy to make time to visit you. The first week of next month looks good for me – which day suits you?

STEVE: I could only make it on the 21st.

ME: OK then, I'm writing down . . . 10 o'clock . . . on the 21st . . . at your offices. I'll send you a brief note now to confirm the appointment and that gives you my phone and fax numbers. My name again is Michael Roe, that's R – O – E, from Research International. I look forward to meeting you on the 21st. Goodbye!

Commentary – a difficult customer, but not unreasonable. After all he thinks he knows my agency and has a perfectly satisfactory current supplier. But I must not let that influence me – I believe in my product and I believe that he can only gain by getting to know about it too. After all, I'm not asking him to buy it, just to become informed. On that premise, I push hard for the meeting. All three objections raised are accepted without argumentation or contradiction, but then I immediately return to my own agenda, which is to get that appointment. At the second objection point, when he raises the issue of cost, I know I will win because he has joined in a discussion and that means we have 'contact' and that he is interested, at however low a level. (I switched to his Christian name quickly after he stated that he had already worked with my company, on the grounds of this representing some familiarity.)

3 Miss Very Busy

Prospect – Teresa Taylor, research manager, Diamond Distilleries
Background – international marketing of spirits
Assumed need – an agency that can handle multinational studies
Benefit – my company can!

ME: Good afternoon, Teresa. This is Michael Roe speaking, executive director of the market research agency Research International – I assume you've heard of us?

TERESA: Look, I'm very busy right now and research is not my priority . . .

ME: Of course, I understand, I would have been fortunate indeed to call just when you were dealing with a research issue, but our new international advertising testing service could be really useful for you because it helps you select the best execution and I wanted to come and tell you about it so that when the need arises you'll know what's available – tell me, are mornings or afternoons generally better for you?

TERESA: I really can't spare the time. I think it would be much better if you simply send me something about it in the post.

ME: Well, I'd like to do that, but you see the best ad testing methods like ours are customized to answer the specific objectives of our clients in each market in which they operate, and when we meet you can tell me your own specific objectives and I can show you how it would be adapted for you – tell me, Teresa, is early or late in the week generally better for you?

TERESA: Look my diary is just impossible in the next few months, what with annual plans, our international meeting, and holidays . . .

ME: I quite understand, but why don't we just pencil in something long term to cover a date in advance. I've got my diary open for three months ahead and if we pencil in an appointment then, let's say the morning of the 25th November, I can contact you again nearer that time and see if you're still available. I'll drop you a line now with my phone and fax numbers, so you can always contact me.

TERESA: The 25th is possible at the moment, but . . .

ME: Right then, can I write in . . . 2.00 p.m . . . on the 25th November . . . at your offices? And then I'll call a week or so before to confirm.

TERESA: Well it's very tentative.

ME: No problem. I'll be in touch with you before then. Good luck with your budget meeting. Looking forward to meeting you in November. Goodbye.

Commentary – delay is the prospect's weapon, probably genuine. But that must not defeat me. I don't care about delay because I know that any appointment I can make is real, however far in the future, and once in a diary one never drops out, however many postponements you may face. Because, simply, the prospect can never admit that he or she was bamboozled into making an appointment they did not want, and pride will demand that they go through with it.

4 Mr Dubious

Prospect – John Wilkerson, marketing manager, Spherical Design Ltd
Background – a medium sized graphical design agency
Assumed need – unsure
Benefit – ?

ME: Good morning, John, my name is Michael Roe, and I'm a director at Research International, the country's leading market research agency. I was wondering if you've heard of us?

JOHN: No I haven't. We don't often get involved in research.

ME: Well, Research International has considerable expertise in packaging design research, enabling you to select the best execution which could be very valuable to you and your clients and that's what I'd like to come and present to you – tell me, John, would a morning or an afternoon suit you better?

JOHN: Well, I think you're far too big and sophisticated for our type of clients. Our budgets are small.

ME: I understand that, John, but in fact we have all kinds of clients, from local to multinational, and we do research projects starting from a few thousands of pounds, and that's what I'd like to tell you about when we meet – would you prefer a morning or afternoon?

JOHN: Well, save yourself the trouble – just put your brochure in the post to me.

ME: I'd be happy to do that, but I'm sure you'll understand that a general brochure can't really show you how our new services would be customized to your particular needs, so I'd be quite happy to make time available to come and see you – how about a date early next month, maybe the 3rd?

JOHN: There nothing relevant on the go at the moment, so you'd be wasting your time.

ME: Thanks for the information, but obviously from what you've just said research needs do sometimes come up, so I think it would be useful for you to know of our services in advance for when the need arises. So maybe we could have a brief meeting on the 3rd?

JOHN: It'll have to be at the end of the day then.

ME: That's fine – so I'm writing in my diary . . . 5.00 p.m. on . . . Wednesday 3rd January . . . at your offices? I'll drop you a line with my name, phone and fax numbers so you can contact me if necessary. Looking forward to the 3rd. Goodbye.

Commentary – not likely to become a large buyer, but my homework showed him to have a good client list, so even if he doesn't commission anything, he may lead me to bigger fish from his own portfolio. Having decided that he is of interest to me I was not going to let him escape by claiming to be small and unimportant. Maybe I could even have used more flattery by showing him how interesting I, from the blue-chip world, found his small business. As with Case 3 – no intention of putting a brochure in the post!

5 Mr Nasty

Prospect – Dominic Dalton, an American, European marketing director, of
    Anglo Automotive Inc
Background – US supplier of automotive parts to auto manufacturers and the
    after market
Assumed need – occasional studies among customers
Benefit – we can do that

ME: Good afternoon Mr Dalton. My name is Michael Roe and I'm CEO of the leading European market research company Research International. Have you heard of us Mr Dalton?

DALTON: No. Why? Should I have?

ME: No reason at all, but I'd like to change that because I think our new research service which provides you with an Automobile Choice Index for Anglo Automotive and your competitors could be very valuable, and that's what . . .

DALTON: Let me just stop you right there, and ask you what you're selling?

ME: Nothing Mr Dalton. I'd simply like to meet you and show you how our service works and how it can benefit you?

DALTON: And is that going to be any better than what we have already?

ME: Well, that'll be for you to judge after we've met, so in general would a morning or an afternoon be better for you?

DALTON: Neither. I could use up all my time if I agreed to see everyone who called me for an appointment.

ME: I understand your difficulty, Mr Dalton, but my feeling was that you should be informed of something as relevant as our Locator model of automobile choice, and that's what I'd like to tell you about when we meet, so would . . .

DALTON: I leave the research details to my product manager.

ME: Well, I'd be quite happy to explain our service to both of you or to him; would some time early next month be convenient?

DALTON: You'd better talk to Victor Lewis about that – I'll transfer you.

(transfer)

ME: Victor, hello. This is Michael Roe, CEO of Research International, the market research agency. I was just talking to Dominic and he asked me to fix up an appointment with you to present our Locator model of automobile purchase – do mornings or afternoons generally suit you better?

VIC: Dominic said that did he. Well, let me see in my diary . . .

APPOINTMENT ACHIEVED

Commentary – difficult contacts are the exception, and in fact Dalton is not particularly difficult, just blunt. (If you are unfortunate enough ever to get a real nasty – then just abort; there are other fish in the sea.) I quote Dalton as an example to illustrate certain aspects of prospection. First – as long as you are having a conversation (not a monologue), as long as the phone is not slammed down on you (which it never is), as long as you keep your cool, remain polite, don't argue, believe in what you are offering, and keep to your objective – to make that appointment – you will succeed! Second – being passed on down the line is not a sign of failure, but provides an enhanced opportunity for success – Vic could not refuse me after my white lie about why Dalton transferred the call. (Note my, quite permissible, adaptation of my own job title to that of CEO, one that is more familiar to Americans.)

Review

The five examples above have been chosen to represent a variety of situations in which the prospector may find him or herself, and to illustrate some of the principal rules of prospecting. What lessons should you learn from them? Here are ten key points:

1 Stick to your script . . .
2 . . . but remain flexible in its application. The words used in the examples do vary slightly from case to case; you will adjust both the phrasing and the words of your script to something you are comfortable with yourself. But the underlying philosophy of approach should remain the backbone.
3 Roll with any objections, 'I'm glad you raised that point' is almost your response, . . . and then return to your own agenda.
4 Arranging that appointment – that's your one and only acceptable close. After every objection you come back to it; it may seem unrelenting and even harsh, but there can be no harm in allowing our prospect to understand that there is no escape – you are determined. Remind yourself – 'I really can help' – in case you worry about the pressure you are exerting.
5 Don't argue; stay polite.
6 Don't invite rejection. Don't ask 'can I come and see you?' Assume the visit is a given. It is only a matter of when. So the question is 'so would a morning or afternoon generally be better for you?'
7 As long as you're both talking you have contact and there has to be some, however flickering, interest from the other party – so persevere and you'll get to your close.
8 Don't make your sales pitch on the phone; keep your ammunition dry for the meeting. But make the benefit of your offer crystal clear to the prospect, not just the features – you have to attract his or her interest, so keep using the 'you' word and the 'new' word.
9 Never agree to put anything in the post – except the confirmation of the appointment.
10 Spell out slowly and precisely the full details of the final appointment being made, as if you are writing it carefully down in your diary – which, of course, you are.

Absorb these lessons and you will find yourself on the long and winding cold canvass trail as illustrated in my case study on the final pages of this chapter.

More sample prospections

Before that, let's face up to the possible barriers of (i) the secretary and (ii) voicemail. Assume Dominic Dalton had a secretary who intercepts your attempt to reach him:

SEC: Mr Dalton's office.

ME: Yes, could I speak to him please.

SEC: What is it concerning?

ME: I just need to have a brief word with him.

SEC: Does he know you?

ME: My name is Michael Roe, and I'm managing director of the market research company Research International. Could you put me through please.

SEC: Well, he's very busy today – my advice would be for you to write to him.

ME: Gladly, but do you know whether he's aware of the problems nowadays with multivariate neural network solutions?

SEC: I'm not sure about that . . .

ME: You see if I could just have a brief word with him about how we can help in this area.

SEC: I'm afraid Mr Dalton is busy right now.

ME: When would be a good time to have a quick word with him on this topic?

SEC: Well, you could try at about 3 o'clock this afternoon

ME: I'll do as you suggest.

Commentary – chances of success remain low here, but if you come across the secretary again when you call back in the afternoon you can imply that she had invited you to recontact at that time and would be untrue to her word if she did not now put you through to Dalton himself. Throughout the earlier conversation you have been insistent but never rude. Your aim has been not to reply directly to her questions when they would lead you to admit weakness (like admitting that you don't actually know Dalton), to stress your seniority, and to move the questioning from her to you, putting her on the defensive. The use of pseudo-science is part of this game plan.

Now let's assume Dalton is protected by voicemail and it seems impossible to reach him directly:

First call

RECORDING: . . . please leave your message now.

ME: Good afternoon Mr Dalton, my name is Michael Roe and I'm executive director of Europe's largest market research agency, called Research International. I've been trying to get in touch with you recently to tell you about our new automobile choice model which I think could be of tremendous value to you and your organization, providing you with just those crucial indices you need. That's what I would like to come and tell you about at a convenient time for you, so I'd be most grateful if you could give me a call to fix an appointment. Let me give you my details – that's Michael Roe, spelt R – O – E, at Research International in London on 0171 656 5000; I'll just repeat that number – 0171 656 5000. I'm looking forward to hearing from you. In case you're too busy to call, I'll recontact you at the same time next week on the chance of reaching you directly. Thank you, Mr Dalton.

No return contact

Second call (at precisely the time and date promised)

RECORDING: . . . please leave your message now.

ME: Good afternoon Mr Dalton, this is Michael Roe from Research International again. You will have received my message last week, but you've probably been too busy to fix a meeting for me to show you our automotive choice model, giving you those vital indices which I know can be of great benefit to you and your company. I myself have been busy during the last week presenting it to some other interested multinationals, and it aroused very positive reactions. I got around to most of them despite that terrible weather we've been having, which caused me problems on the M1. Anyway, I would really like to come and talk to you about it at a convenient time for you, so I'd be most grateful if you could give me a call to fix an appointment. Let me give you my details again – that's Michael Roe, spelt R – O – E, at Research International in London on 0171 656 5000; I'll just repeat that number – 0171 656 5000. I'm looking forward to hearing from you. In case you're too busy to call, I'll recontact you at the same time next week in the chance of reaching you directly. Thank you, Mr Dalton.

No contact

Third call (at precisely the time and date promised)

RECORDING: . . . please leave your message now.

ME: Good afternoon Mr Dalton, this is Michael Roe from Research International once again. Still battling my way around the country to meet all those requests for a presentation of our new automotive choice model. I do hope you and I can fix one up soon. Please do give me a call, here are my details again . . . If you're too busy to call, I'll contact you again same time next week . . .

If necessary – fourth call (at precisely the time and date promised)

. . . and so on

Commentary – what more can I say? Can he resist? Will he call? Or will he be annoyed? Try it for yourself. Voicemail problems will increase and we will all need to perfect our methods to overcome it. The above is not fully proven but worth a trial.

Case study
From shirts to soups via most of the UK

A prospection trail

The objective – to win a major new client for a London-based market research agency.

The saga begins with me spotting a news item in the trade press referring to a market research officer at a Courtaulds office in Nottingham. A check of our client records confirmed that no contact existed with Courtaulds, which, as a major UK corporation, offered the opportunity of a sizeable new business prospect.

Using Directory Enquiries and with help from switchboard staff, the researcher was tracked down and the first, really cold, prospection call made to fix an appointment to present my company to him in Nottingham. The standard script was used, no objections raised, and the meeting fixed – all over within seconds. Success at Round 1.

Most of a day was invested in the trip from London to Nottingham which took place about one month later. It transpired that the researcher was working in one division of the Courtaulds' empire, branded shirts, which had a very limited budget, and focused most of his attention on the analysis of internal statistics. A friendly meeting, but on the drive back down to London the distinct impression of a day wasted.

This impression remained as the weeks turned into months and nothing further was heard. Until a call came in after three months. It was from the prospect but now at a different location. He had been transferred to the Courtaulds London HQ, controlling a larger budget and would I like to come in and receive a competitive brief! Success at Round 2.

The brief was received and the proposal delivered – but the tender lost on price to the competition. Failure at Round 3. (Relative failure: obviously my agency would be on the shortlist for further briefs in the future.)

A further lengthy interval now occurs. The next incident again derives from the trade press: it is announced that the prospect has been appointed as market research manager for Scottish & Newcastle Breweries in Edinburgh. A quick call, definitely under the 'warm' category, and within weeks the journey north is made again to present the agency's specific alcoholic drinks research expertise.

At this meeting the ricochet technique is employed. The prospect is happy to divulge the name of his ad agency planner (fortunately in London.) This warm lead is very quickly followed up and produces the anticipated easy appointment at CDP Advertising. Success at Round 4.

Which allows a speedy repeat circuit around the sales referral technique: a good meeting at CDP produces the second research brief of this case study. Interestingly enough it does not come from Scottish & Newcastle – no further is heard from them – but from another CDP client, Harvey's of Bristol, the sherry company. Our name has been recommended to them by CDP as a result of the recent pitch, and they ask me to visit them for a briefing on a small NPD project.

By this time therefore, the new business team has been to Nottingham, Edinburgh, and now Bristol; over nine months have elapsed since the first prospecting call; no business has been won, but the second brief is to hand. Success at Round 5.

Pyrrhic? Definitely not. I win this small bid. Success at Round 6. Real money is now changing hands.

And the saga continues. In working with Harvey's, we come in contact with a local Bristol design agency who have good contacts with a client operating from offices in the same street as Harvey's, namely the large supermarket chain Gateway (today renamed Somerfield). One of the design team is in the process of transferring to Gateway and is soon involved in recommending us to bid for a major research project. Gateway is planning to set up a continuous new product evaluation system for all its own-label products, from soups to soaps. At last, the trail has lead to a significant opportunity – this project is wc rth over £250 000 on a contractual, annual basis.

It is won after a lengthy series of competitive pitches. It represents the largest single win in my career as business development director. Final success at Round 7. Champagne!

But it was not to be. Before the system could begin to be implemented, the client was subject to a hostile take-over bid, everything went on hold and then into abeyance as the take-over succeeded and the existing management ousted. Our project hit the dustbin. Now victory was indeed Pyrrhic; but for the new business director it went into the books as a 'success without victory'.

Chapter 6

Being there!
Cold canvass
presenting and
pitching

Once again, my advice derives from my own hard, practical experience and is addressed to all those in professional services. There are three distinct situations that need to be isolated: (1) The credentials presentation, i.e. cold canvass (following successful prospecting as described in the previous chapter); and (2) The pitch for business, i.e. tendering (usually in response to a specific client brief and mostly in a competitive context). And then I will deal with (3) The written proposal document.

I The cold canvass credentials presentation

When this lies before you, the mood should be one of exhilaration and excitement. At last you are face to face with your target. This has been your ultimate objective, based on the confident expectation that professional to professional you will give it your best shot and succeed. If you do not feel this will be so, it may be asked why you have been given/taken on the sales role in the first place. Success may not be immediate, it may not take the form you might expect or be of a size to match your optimistic forecasts, but the chance, the strike rate, is high – higher than from any other form of marketing. And you have brought this opportunity about either directly by your own prospection or indirectly through your marketing activities. The fish is there under your rod, you just need to choose the right bait and it will in most probability bite. With good preparation and follow-through execution the chance becomes higher still, multiplied by repeat business opportunities, so let's consider the checklist of preparations and actions.

I The visit

If possible, two representatives from your organization should attend. Since personal chemistry is always a crucial element in any relationship, this provides you with two bites at the cherry. Further contact may be pursued by the one who felt the greatest affinity with the client or could better offer the requisite experience and/or expertise. It also permits one of you to focus attention on the prospect while the other is busy presenting, allowing the former to spot signs that may lead to a change of focus or emphasis as the presentation proceeds. The speaker/presenter is usually so involved in his or her speech that they may fail to pick up or be sensitive to slight indications from the client of particular interest or doubt. These may come from body language as well as actual language, and you or your colleague could intervene with a phrase such as 'it seemed to me that the issue of XYZ which we only briefly touched upon, might be of more interest to you than . . .'

Remember the visit is more than just the period of time when you and the prospect are closeted together in a room. It begins with the homework you have done before you start your journey. It continues with any considerate behaviour you may reveal if you are running late. Even as you wait in the foyer it is surprising how much useful detail you can pick up: the in-house magazine is a source of real detail; the plaque on the wall announcing ISO registration; the POS material on display to inform staff of an upcoming product launch; etc. And it all starts in earnest with the introductory handshake. It never fails to surprise me how much can still be learnt during the walk with the prospect to the meeting room; this need not be just small talk – you can refer to what you saw in the foyer and will probably learn a lot more. You may pick up personal details about the prospect that can be used later, e.g. hobbies and interests that can provide an excuse for a follow-up call. Again, the same applies as you leave – the conversation as you walk back to reception can provide further insights.

Surprises may occur, and are usually positive – 'I've invited my boss to join us as she's very interested in XYZ'; 'I know you said you were going to tell me about XYZ, but if we've got time, could you also cover ABC?'; 'When we've finished, my colleague wonders if you could just spare a few moments to discuss a particular issue he is wrestling with?' Great! However, if it's 'I'm very sorry, but I've got to rush to another meeting in ten minutes' then live with it, take a minute to compose yourself, and deliver your one key message – and don't overrun.

2 Equipment

Until recently it was said that a professional presentation demanded the use of 35 mm slides. These were certainly superior to paper flipcharts. Since it was unlikely that one could demand the provision of projector and darkened conference room for what is often a meeting of fewer than four persons, a wonderful solution was provided by the Kindermann portable slide projector. With an in-built back-projection screen it is a truly desktop machine and can be set up and put into action within a few minutes of arriving, using any office surface as its base and without the need to reduce ambient lighting. The only limitation is the size of the screen, which implies a maximum audience of about five persons.

Today, the Kindermann is replaced by the laptop ... or should be! Surprisingly, many are reluctant to use these machines during a visit. They tend to restrict its use to database building and contact management rather than for selling itself. This is a pity since it denies the salesperson the power and potential it can bring to face-to-face selling – the impact of PowerPoint charts, photos, videos, etc. all available at a click; coupled with the aura of modernity and professionalism. Of course, it should be done without ever allowing the Windows or applications loading to be seen, and this is quite easy with modern software, e.g. LapTop Navigator from Imarco. And add an LCD projector (e.g. Philips Impact desktop version) for an audience of more than two.

3 The art of listening

Dialogue not monologue! You've come to do your presentation, and your natural instinct will drive you to deliver that presentation, come what may. The danger is monologue, with no real human contact, just your single-minded gabble. Remember a motherhood statement on selling:

Selling should be 75 per cent listening and 25 per cent talking

Why not start the conversation off with these words – 'I've got a considerable amount of interesting material with me, but maybe I can focus it better onto your specific needs if you could kick off by telling me what issues are particularly concerning you at this moment'. Prospects are usually only too keen to have an audience for their problems and, as they talk, you can be re-ordering your pitch to target even better.

40 per cent hear through their eyes

20 per cent respond from their ears

40 per cent react from their feelings

Words alone are probably not enough. Your appearance and your manner (both of you, if you are a pair) have a massive effect. Appearance is for you to judge,

I cannot pronounce without knowing your market – is it formal or casual? With regard to manner, it is obvious that you must be confident and positive. You are the professional, so be professional. You know your business inside out – you shouldn't be in front of the prospect if you don't. You should be able to make an excellent presentation in your sleep. The equipment you may have brought is an aid, not a prop.

But don't be complacent or arrogant. You are the visitor, the guest, the invitee – never forget it, and show by your manner that you haven't forgotten it.

Whatever the subject, the client (and his/her personality) is the object

This is a blind date. Since the prospection call was in all probability very brief, you have little forewarning of the character and personality of the prospect. You must be adaptable.

Talking of the personality of the prospect, in her book *Selling Professionally* (Kogan Page, 1991), Rebecca Morgan refers to four main personality types you may meet and their attributes, to which you must adapt during the meeting. In summary:

1 The Detail Seeker – always asks 'how?', needs precision, fears criticism.
2 The Results Seeker – asks 'what?' and 'when?', needs power and authority, fears being taken advantage of.
3 The Excitement Seeker – asks 'who?', needs public recognition and fears loss of same
4 The Harmony Seeker – asks 'why?', needs security and the status quo, fears loss of security.

What more is there to say? You have to get the chemistry to work. Don't assume you're on trial, meeting resistance, wasting time. It is far more likely that the prospect is genuinely interested, wants to engage in dialogue, and poses questions out of real interest and not aggression. You will certainly find you have spent more time with the prospect doing the presentation than you ever would have dared request at the moment of the prospecting call. Valuable information will be provided to you spontaneously – use it, i.e. as soon as you're out of the building write it all down.

4 Sell the benefit NOT the features or technique

Another motherhood statement, but one that can never be over-emphasized. There is the terrible temptation to talk about what interests you, i.e. the features/the mechanics, rather than the benefit that should accrue to the client. As a professional, features interest you. As a potential buyer, the prospect may share your interests – but equally may solely be interested in the end result. It is your job to make that benefit clear and unambiguous – '. . . and this is what you get' rather than '. . . and this is what we do.' For many clients, the mechanics may comfortably remain a black box, only to be opened if requested.

Let me give an example of putting this approach into action; it requires a lateral mindset.

My agency had a centre for telephone research, a rapidly growing sector for market research data collection. Since it had reached capacity, we moved to a brand new centre, renewing all our equipment and doubling the number of telephone stations from forty to eighty. Naturally we planned a marketing push to launch the new centre.

How would we mark this event? We thought of a drinks party at the centre, to which we would invite both existing clients and prospects. What would the invitation feature – 'Come and see our new telephone research centre'. A logical approach.

Not really. We were featuring the mechanic not the benefit. Putting ourselves into the shoes of the client raised a number of questions – 'Why should I come?'; 'What's so interesting?'; 'Is there anything unique to see?'. Our own answers were depressing – the centre was no better, no larger, no more high tech than others available. Yes it was nice and new, it was important to us – but why should that interest the client?

Now it so happened that, coincidentally, during about the same period our agency was launching a really unique new technique, called The Equity Engine, which offered clients the benefit of being able for the first time to obtain a simple index measure of their own and their rivals' brand equity. Data for this model could be collected either by face to face or telephonic means from respondents.

Here was an opportunity to offer a real benefit, on the coat tails of which the telephone centre could be launched. The cover of the invitation said – 'Discover how to measure your brand equity on the telephone' and inside 'A new technique in a new telephone centre' with the announcement of a presentation about the Equity Engine to be held at the new telephone centre. Here was a reason to attend.

So always adopt the 'laddering' approach, moving from feature to benefit with transitions such as –

'. . . and this provides you with . . .'

'. . . which means you'll be able to . . .'

'. . . allowing you and your company to . . .'

Try it out, practise, with all your services, always remembering to use the 'you' or 'your company' words for that personal focus. It's all about reassurance and keeping things simple.

5 'Consultative selling'

This technique is the subject of its own book, written by Eric Baron of CRC, Darien, Connecticut, USA. I recommend it as a guide to controlling the presentation process, and the barest outline is provided here, which never-theless reveals his method's key means and intent.

Eric defines the basic aim of his technique as follows: 'My overall objective is to bring a problem-solving approach to the sales process. The competitive environment in which we find ourselves demands that anyone responsible for developing business must act as a problem-solving resource to the client in order to differentiate themselves from the competition.'

What he goes on to do is to place the Problem-Solving sequence (i.e. how we should approach problem-solving situations) alongside the Needs-Driven Selling sequence (i.e. how to draw out needs from clients) to show how the two have considerable similarities which will allow them to be merged.

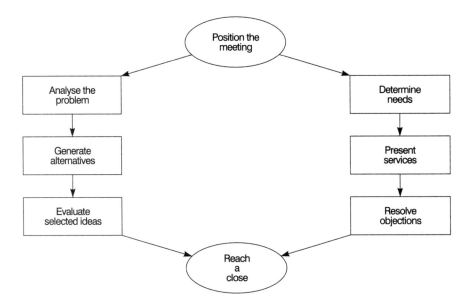

The left-hand column represents the Problem-Solving sequence; the right-hand the Needs Driven. To 'analyse the problem' and 'determine needs' he recommends the systematic asking of questions and listening to the answers in order to find the link with your services so you can present.

There are four stages to the consultative selling approach which merges these two sequences:

1 Opening
2 Needs determination
3 Presentation
4 Closing

The opening aims to set the climate and allows you to state your own objectives for the meeting: 'What I thought would interest you is . . .' Immediately it moves on to a listening phase whereby the prospect is allowed his or her own input, after which you return to restate the objectives (now joint) and break them into components: 'So as I understand it what you'd like me to focus on will be . . .' The presentation then proceeds, alert all the time for response and eager to engage in conversation rather than just monologue. Finally, you move to the close, the subject of my next section. Here is a summary of the process –

1 **Opening** – position the meeting, put the client at ease, set the climate and state your objective, e.g. '*What I thought would interest you is* . . .'The objective here is to establish rapport and confirm objectives that can be held in common.
2 **Needs determination** – analyse the situation, redefine and break into components, e.g. '*So as I understand it, what you would like me to focus on will be* . . .' Having gained a response to your opening, you have taken on board the prospect's wishes and restated the needs/opportunities.
3 **Present** – offer recommendations using benefits not features, and keep listening out for needs, e.g. '*You seemed to be particularly interested in* . . .'
4 **Close** – draw out/reframe/address objections, e.g. '*Where do we go from here?*'You must resolve any objections satisfactorily and then move on to establishing next steps and planning the follow up. You do not expect to close with a sale; you do expect to emerge from the presentation with a clear plan for continuation of the contact.

This structure should have been planned before your visit.

6 Closing the presentation

Once again it must be emphasized that you are not in one of those high-powered 'CLOSE THAT SALE!' situations. You don't expect that sort of decision from prospects who are professionals. What you do expect is a pause for thought, gestation, and, at some future date, the arrival of the moment of need – at which time you must be remembered. You can't close now because this need may not yet be present.

Closing in such a situation must be a joint exercise between you and the prospect: ensure that any objections that may exist have been drawn out, possibly reframed, and certainly dealt with. Then you may even pose the question: 'Where do we go from here?' Often the expectation can be no more than the acceptance and agreement on the prospect's part to get in touch when the need/opportunity arises. You should feel comfortable that you have given it your best shot, addressed the prospect's most pressing issues in a confident and relevant manner. Hopefully the prospect will feel that something useful has been learnt and that another potential supplier has been added to the roster.

At this point the handing over of a visiting card and brochure(s) is important; not in the expectation that the latter will be read, but to act as a memory jog. One trick that may be used here is to deliberately – but unknown to the prospect – keep back one brochure (on the assumption that you have more than one). It provides you with a future follow-up opportunity: 'following our discussions it occurred to me that you might be interested in this. It wasn't available at the time we met so I am forwarding it to you now.' A white lie, but quite acceptable.

Make copious notes immediately you leave. They will provide the basis for any follow-up activity. Keeping in touch is a necessity but far from easy to achieve (see below). It will not be possible to simply call and request an explanation from the prospect as to why you have not yet received a brief/commission! Your notes may help: was a new development date referred to that could be used as a peg for a recall? A change in responsibilities? You will have to use your judgement. Secondly, these notes will, of course, become your database.

A sample record form might look as follows:

Record Sheet – Visit

Prospect name	_____		
Designation	_____		
Title	_____		
Company	_____		
Phone no.	_____		
Fax no.	_____		
	SERVICES PRESENTED		
APPOINTMENT	Date _____	Time _____	Others present? _____
NOTES FOR MEETING			
Follow-up plan			

. . . and please don't forget to ask for a referral (remember the 'ricochet' method in the Preparation section of the previous chapter).

7 The follow up

How will you follow through, and when? Given that the gestation period for a pitch can be years, there can be no clear answer to this problem. The 'missing' brochure can be sent off, along with your 'thank you' letter within a few weeks of the presentation; but as to further action, subjective views rule.

One thing is certain – if you do nothing you will be victim of the '2' Rule:

You have 2 'hello . . .' calls

You have 2 months to anonymity

So act. Set up a 'tickler' or 'suspense' file, divided into months, into which you can place your reminders. Look at it in good time. Then you must make a reason to call. Here are some suggestions:

● send details of a new product or service
● send a relevant case study
● send a new brochure
● send any relevant press cutting
● send a client win notification
● invite to a seminar
● send some interesting information about their competition

Use any method you can think of to remain top of mind.

Patience

Now you are at the end of the 3 'P' cycle – Prepare; Prospect; Present. Sit back and wait for success!?! Yes, it will come; no, it's a numbers game and you need to repeat the process endlessly.

The outline of this chapter does not refer to the topic of reward/success and the time it might take. Focus is on method; the successful end result is taken for granted. You are now entitled to have your spirits raised in order to commit with enthusiasm to the rigours of the method, where fear has been clearly accepted as a major barrier.

The case study at the end of the previous chapter should act as a spur, although it is a uniquely long drawn out success story, a tribute to perseverance/patience with a bitter/sweet reward. At this point it may be useful to provide more direct reassurance.

● **Prospection**: just hit your first target of the day and adrenaline will drive you on to many more; the power of success never fails to amaze, so you must press on until you gain that first appointment/brief/win because after that the will to go further will be irresistible.

- **Prospection**: with perseverance, you will soon reach the point where three-quarters of your effective prospecting calls will get an appointment. Such a success rate should not be compared with the much lower effectivity of telephone sales – you are not selling anything other than an appointment, so the risk the prospect is taking is reduced.
- **Presentation**: eventually, you will look back at your records and find that at least one-third of all your presentation visits will have led to the receipt of a brief – i.e. success, since a brief is an opportunity to win new business (your ability to convert these into actual business is not germane at this point).
- **Presentation**: don't judge by appearances, either going in to do your pitch or upon exiting. You'll probably be wrong – the grumpiest target is just as likely to become your best client and the friendliest never heard from again. Treat all equally – you never know from where the job will finally come.
- Over a longer time period you will detect a 'snowball' effect as: your name is passed on to others; your prospect turns up at a new position; you are invited back to talk to colleagues of the original prospect; etc.
- A response after a two-year interval is by no means unusual. There is no greater feeling than to pick up the telephone and hear: 'Good morning, you may remember that some little while ago you came to tell me about your services. Well I've got a brief here that might interest you . . .' Shout it out aloud! This is what it is all about. What happens next is irrelevant. Of course, there is still work to be done to win the job. But you can even try to claim success in its absence. In other words, briefs not converted into wins are no different from those won for the business development director since his or her task is predicated on providing new business *opportunities* – their conversion into business is not the primary issue!

Keep alert for 'hidden' success. Clients have notoriously bad memories, and it is frequently the case that they will follow up your pitch after an interval but with poor recall of your name. The call could come in to your company with no recipient specified and so be snaffled by a colleague.

Results and rewards

'If you tell me what you measure and reward, I'll tell you your strategy . . . because I'll be able to tell you what your people will go out and do'

David Maister

All this prospection and selling is nothing if it does not deliver results for your organization and reward for yourself.

For your organization, you must insist/demand at the outset that they give you a nine-month new business warm-up period before results are analysed; time in which to conduct all your preparations and get a solid block of, say fifty, presentations behind you. For this brief period only will you be an overhead; later, you will pay for yourself out of your new business successes. Beyond that, argue to have a bonus reward formula based on new business success.

But what to class as success? I make a strong claim that a new business function should be judged on the basis of opportunities created, that conversion is another issue. This is particularly the case when you are delegating briefs that come in from your sales pitches. If you are spreading these around the organization to those best equipped to handle them, then you are no longer in control of your own destiny and could be judged on the basis of RFPs (Request For Proposal) alone.

But it is doubtful you will win the argument that your task stops at the provision of new business opportunities (no hard-nosed MD will be prepared to count 'potential pounds' – they want real ones!) It is still worth keeping a record of both wins and losses. And push hard to have repeat business recognized. I have had very lengthy discussions with my own chairman as to when I should cease to take repeat business into my sales figures. We began with his opening gambit of the first three jobs; I countered with a claim for a three-year limit (irrespective of number of jobs). It started to get more complicated when the issue arose of annual contracts from clients – were these single jobs? I must leave you to fight your own battles.

Here is a real-life example of how such a three-year analysis might look:

	Presentations	Won	Lost
Year 1	73	£220 000	£125 000
Year 2	67	£350 000	£230 000
Year 3	45	£875 000	£450 000
Years 4+	combination of new wins and repeat business averaging over £600 000		

Notes: Average size of job £30 000; decline in number of pitches due to inability to delegate in all cases; includes up to first three jobs only from any new client; some year 3 wins come from year 1/2 pitches.

Over £1 million in bid **opportunities** by Year 3! Every pound on the list through your own efforts! Probably thousands of prospection calls; hundreds of visits – but a million in reward. And the reward certainly more than covers your time and cost, because, if your professional service is as good as you must believe it is, then the money comes from satisfied clients who will buy again and again. So go for it! It works!

What about calculating the monetary benefit to your organization. Here's how I justified/magnified (choose your verb!) the value I was bringing in, using a theoretical example that is not far from the achievable reality. My organization talks in terms of gross margin, GM; yours may refer to gross profit or use some other term. What it refers to is income minus variable/out-of-pocket costs. I set my GM in sales against total company GM, assuming that no extra staff are required to perform the additional work my sales bring in. So I considered four columns for analysis:

1 Current – situation before salesperson's cost
2 First Step – salesperson's cost but as yet no income
3 Next Step – GM income from sales equals salesperson's cost times three
4 Final Step – gearing reaches factor of four

	£'000			
	1 Current	*2 + Cost*	*3 + Sales × 3*	*4 + Sales × 4*
Gross margin	2000	2000	2150	2200
Fixed operational costs	(1600)	(1650)	(1650)	(1650)
... of which salesperson	0	(50)	(50)	(50)
Profit	400	350	500	550

I submit that these figures look excellent! Profit increase against current at column 3 is 25 per cent and by column 4 reaches 38 per cent, set against the initial risk of investment with the early no income situation temporarily reducing profits by minus 12 per cent in column 2 (resulting from a 3 per cent increase in costs). On this basis I believe your organization could afford to bonus you at 10 per cent of the GM of your new business for any sales which exceed £100 000 (i.e. after covering your costs and delivering some extra profit for the organization)!

2 The new business pitch against a brief (beauty parade)

All the above advice remains in force plus some further elements detailed below. But overriding everything is the question of mood – winning is the only acceptable outcome; you are not selling a meeting any more so there is no point whatever in coming second. It is easy to, but you must not, prepare yourself for losing – it will show. So what else is there?

In contrast to the credentials presentation, which is usually fixed format with the content decided by you in part, the competitive pitch is led by the client brief. Since this should be received in advance, the advice can be split between what to do *before* the pitch and what to do *during*. The points are made as succinctly as possible so as to act as a checklist. Of course, all pitches are not the same, but the principles remain.

Before the pitch . . .

- Clarify and (if necessary) challenge the brief now. Ideally it should be a written brief. Make sure you understand it. If not, telephone for clarification and write down the answers. If you disagree with something, now is the time to (try to) change the client's mind. The same applies if you think the timing plan is unrealistic. And try to get an idea of their budget!
- Determine their attendees and time schedule(s); check availability of presentation equipment (OHP; 35 mm: LCD projector; flipcharts) – if in doubt, take your own; how large is the room? – affects size of chart text and voice projection.
- Plan your team (who attends and who presents) in response and appoint a team leader. Try not to outnumber the clients. Draw up a timetable and stick to it. Agree dress code.
- Send your team CVs in advance together with any background literature, plus confirmation of date, time and venue. Decide what you're going to leave behind after the pitch.
- Try to establish who your competition are and prepare comparisons with yourselves. If possible, try to be the last to present.
- If travelling there – never get separated from your material; check out the room beforehand.

The pitch – structure and planning

SAY WHAT YOU'RE GOING TO SAY

SAY IT

SAY WHAT YOU'VE SAID

. . . in other words, remove uncertainty at the outset, move on to the detail and then drive the message home via repetition. (Another reason to put a management summary up-front – the key person in your audience, the decision maker, is always at risk of being called out for an urgent reason; so you have to provide a synopsis in the first few minutes that he or she can remember.)

- Give the pitch a title
- Write down in one sentence what you want to get across – i.e. the theme
- Divide the pitch into chapters
- Give a role to each speaker
- Never show an organization chart
- If you will be using case histories, make sure they're not giving away any confidential material
- No lies!
- Prepare/prepare/prepare

- Rehearse/rehearse/rehearse
- Be ready for possible questions; harmonize answers

... and throughout, **show how you can help** (the benefits not the techniques).

Charts

- Be creative
- Keep them simple, clear, uncluttered
- Use them for talking around, not for reading from
- Make effective use of borders, logos, colour, symbols
- Move from using transparencies to an LCD projector as soon as you can
- PowerPoint can be great; even better would be multimedia

During the pitch ...

- Make it interesting
  - do not waffle – keep it simple – remembering the myth that ...

... research proves ...

a speaker has **the whole** of an audience's attention for about ten minutes ...

... **half** their attention for the next ten minutes ...

... and after half an hour **most** of the audience start having sexual fantasies!!

  - keep the focus on the client's business – offer reassurance
  - if you do not make a key point every three minutes the client will lose interest!
  - quality of speech – get the pace right; use pauses effectively; cut out the 'ehs' and 'ums'
  - make sure you can be heard
  - avoid the monotone; use a well-modulated voice
- Body language and eye contact – it is said that the communication of your message is made up of:

58 per cent body – 27 per cent voice – 15 per cent content

- So focus on stance/hands/eyes/voice/nerves.
  - *stance* – stand up straight, don't block their view, try to stand still but if you move, don't sway, avoid 'crutches' (chairs, walls, etc.)
  - *hands* – out of pockets, control 'tics' (scratching, etc.), use gestures well (arm movements mainly)
  - *eyes* – use eye contact (but not shifty, darting eyes), engage different members of the audience but avoid 'flitting' or holding one person's gaze too long

- *voice* – project to suit room, keep it strong right to the end of sentences, not too fast not too slow, vary tone to show interest and enthusiasm
- *nerves* – everybody has them, adrenaline helps a presentation, breathe deeply, nerves abate quickly so rehearse the start particularly well
- No arrogance
- Stick to the timetable
- Show how much you want to work for them – say it
- Listen carefully to anything they might say
- Handle questions by listening carefully, addressing your answer to the whole audience, and deferring those for which you have no immediate answer

At the end of the pitch . . .

- CLOSE – ask for the business.
- Leave something behind – a copy of the presentation OR a brochure OR your visiting cards.
- When you get back to the office – review and judge your performance focusing on areas for improvement.

. . . and if after all this you win it; then celebrate!

'Money, money, money'

A brief word about pricing. Remember:

'sales are vanity; profit is sanity'

. . . so don't underprice!

You are a boutique, not a supermarket. Stress value rather than cost; set client benefits against your price; break price into its constituents (menu pricing) to give the client the opportunity to play with options; if possible, use a Trojan horse as part of your pricing offer – a valued 'extra' at no, or low, cost (but never say 'free'!); and why not utilize M&S-type price points, i.e. $15 900 rather than $16 000? (A round price does after all somewhat contradict your claim to have carefully constructed a unique, detailed solution to the client's unique problem – see below.)

You should be aware of the market segment you are in, and the price level that it justifies, whatever the competition. Defend it. For a salesperson, there is an obvious temptation to discount the first job for a new prospect in order to be able to claim a success. Don't do it. In both cases, once you have lowered your price you will never get it back to a 'proper' level. If pricing becomes an issue, treat it as an 'objection' and handle it in the manner already proposed in the previous chapter for dealing with objections, and/or utilize the consultative selling techniques detailed above.

3 Writing a winning proposal

Not always can the business win be achieved face to face; much business rests on the written proposal or tender, which may be required before or after the pitch or presentation. What advice can be given about the production of such a document? Well, the same principles still apply.

> The primary task of a professional services agency is to guarantee that the client problem is identified, the objectives defined and the means selected are perfectly consistent.

The figure below shows this diagrammatically.

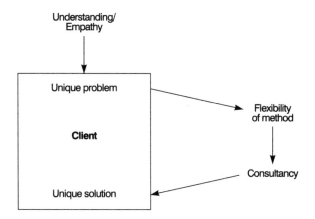

This takes us right back to Chapter 1 and the 'I'm special'/'I can help' relationship. The client wants a customized solution; you usually produce a customized answer. But in the case that you have taken an 'off-the-shelf' answer – you must never make it appear anything other than customized.

Your documentation must take the client through the full consultancy process by indicating empathy with the 'unique' problem, revealing your flexibility of method, your analytical skills – and then presenting the solution as a unique one, consistent with the needs analysis and emphasizing the benefits rather than the features.

According to Aubrey Wilson's *Emancipating the Professions (1994)*, you have five roles which should all feature and show through your document –

1 Consultant
2 Information Provider
3 Problem Solver
4 Professional Partner
5 Negotiator

The resulting document should therefore comprise at least the following sections, with the document itself and the individual parts of indeterminate length (entirely dependent on the size of the job/contract):

● Background information and objectives – *analysis and overview = shows understanding*
● Discussion – *crucial consultancy stage – with assumptions stated, pros and cons of various options considered, and solution chosen for reasons with clear client benefits*
● Solution/Proposition/Methodology – *detailed features of final means chosen to solve problem (keep technical/professional details for appendices)*
● Timing and cost – *should never be final section, nor should costs be left 'naked' on the page, but always set alongside recap of features/benefits, and offering options for negotiation*
● Deliverables – *driving home immediately what they get for their money*
● Credentials – *of your organization*
● Project team – *their titles, roles and CVs*

For larger proposals, you need a contents page and a management summary up-front (for those who will not read the entire document). Make sure your logo is on every page (also scanning in the client logo) and the page numbering system is of the 'Page x of y' type so that no part of the document can be lost. Then proof read, a spell check is not sufficient!

Finally, the document should be written in a style such that the readers can be 'nodding' their heads in agreement as you take them from page to page and, in doing so, unfold your argumentation. And talking of style, make good use of a thesaurus and something like *The Economist Style Guide*. If possible, introduce a graphical visualization of your planned programme of activities – a picture is worth a thousand words and can act as a one-page summary of your entire offer.

Quality of writing varies tremendously. Most professionals think they can write well, but it's not the case. Some hints are provided below derived from Jeremy Stratton in *Professional Marketing* (October 1993):

There are three golden rules to remember:

1 Write from the client's point of view
2 Write from the client's point of view
3 Write from the client's point of view

Some writing techniques:

● put the key points in the first line of each section to encourage people to read on
● never repeat the headline in the first line of text
● you've got 5–10 seconds for your main message to be absorbed

- use simple, clear language
- avoid gender or age bias
- only ask questions to which the reader will reply in the positive
- do not use a negative to illustrate a positive
- use active rather than passive words
- check the friendliness of your work by reading it out aloud – if it sounds stilted, start again
- keep lines to between twenty and sixty characters in length
- make sure YOU is used more frequently than I or WE
- use evocative words to help paint the picture

You must be pro-active throughout the proposal process. Of course, you cannot write your proposal until you have received the RFP (Request For Proposal). When it arrives, your first task is to acknowledge it – simply good manners. And why not acknowledge in style – a written note to the client expressing interest and excitement (the sales process starts right here). Similarly, at the end of the process, why not deliver your proposal personally? What better way can there be to show your enthusiasm? If you are likely to be the more expensive among the bidders, you should make every effort to be given the opportunity to present your proposal in person so that you can defend your price. Should you be unlucky enough to lose the bid, remember that your task is not over; you must make the effort to discover why you have lost in as much detail as the client is prepared to provide. Diagnosis is the key to future success.

There may be occasions when you will decide to decline to bid. Remember, your objective is not simply to win business for your organization but to win *better* business, i.e. more profitable business. Some clients are time wasters, with no intention of changing suppliers and limited long-term potential. Others get a kick out of the sheer number of competing tenders they can induce. You must use your judgement whether or not to enter the ring on all occasions.

Sample cold canvass presentations

Towards the end of the previous chapter I reproduced samples of telephonic interchanges between myself and prospects as a means of indicating the application of the recommended script and objections handling. Here I shall continue with one of these exercises, picking up the characters once more at their point of contact, i.e. at the appointment itself, and providing one right and one wrong cold canvass presentation interaction. At certain moments I shall skip the full detail of the service features and benefits in order to short-cut the text. My aim is to show the use of some of the techniques described in the current chapter, especially the need to focus on benefits, the principles of consultative selling, and classic closing. Again, just substitute your own professional service prospect/offer as you read.

Miss Nice

Prospect – Natalie Smith, director of research, Unigamble plc

Background – Unigamble regularly launch new household cleaning products aimed at housewives

Assumed need – to gain advance information on the likely sales success of new brands

Benefit – my company has a technique which predicts sales volume potential before market launch

Recommended approach

ME: Thank you for making time available to see me out of your busy schedule. I have brought with me presentations of a number of our unique services, but before starting, do you agree that it might be useful for you to tell me a little about what issues are particularly concerning you at the moment regarding research and then I can focus on them?

NATALIE: Yes, I could do that. You see what the company in general and I in particular will be faced with later this year will be ...

ME: That's very interesting. So my understanding from what you've told me is that you would be most interested in brand equity measurement?

NATALIE: Yes, why don't you just show me what you have on that.

ME (SETTING UP BRAND EQUITY PRESENTATION): This seems to be what interests you, how our new technique can provide you with the measures you need. Let me briefly describe how it works, the benefits you get and how you can use the results. This will take about thirty minutes.

NATALIE: That's OK.

ME: Well, ...
....
....

NATALIE: Thank you for that. I think that's all I've time for now.

ME: Are there any elements that are unclear to you?

NATALIE: No, I think I have all the information I need at this moment.

ME: Let me leave you with our brochure for you to refer to, and here is my visiting card. Would you like me to send you those case studies I referred to?

NATALIE: Yes, you could do that.

ME: By the way, who is your ad agency on this brand?

NATALIE: O & M.

ME: I assume they have a planner on your account – do you think he or she might also be interested in this technique?

NATALIE: Why not – it's Stephen Edinburgh there who does our planning.

ME: Thanks for that. I'll get in touch. And I'll contact you later in the year when you said this need might arise. Thank you. Goodbye.

Commentary – basic principles have been followed. I gave Natalie the opportunity to guide the agenda and timing of our meeting (note that the topic eventually covered was not that pitched during the prospecting call), I focused on the benefits, clarified that all was clearly understood at the end of my presentation, created an excuse for follow up, and listened well enough to her own comments to be able to fix a relevant recontact date. I also achieved a referral at the ad agency. So, a successful meeting with a good prognosis on two fronts.

Wrong approach
ME: Well Natalie, as I told you when I called some weeks ago, I want to tell you about our MicroTest technique which I know will be of interest to you. It won't take long and then I'll be on my way. So here goes ...

45 MINUTES LATER

ME: I'm sure you'll agree that that's all very interesting stuff, so thanks for your attention and I'm sure we'll be in contact soon. Goodbye.

Commentary – assuming that she remembered the reason for my visit, I went straight into the presentation without giving her any opportunity for input, or indeed myself a chance to pick up any useful titbits of information. I probably bored the pants off her and then ran out and left her with a poor impression of my consultancy skills. A wasted opportunity.

A few wise words

In this section I have repeatedly referred to one of your tasks as being that of offering your client confidence via your personality and by adopting the KISS mentality (Keep It Simple, Stupid) in your pitch or presentation. The words below were written over 100 years ago by William James, the great American psychologist and philosopher. They reveal the need in all humans for simplicity and reassurance that should guide your approach in face-to-face meetings.

> 'The facts of the world in their sensible diversity are always before
> us, but our theoretic need is that they should be conceived in a way
> that reduces their manifoldness to simplicity. Our pleasure in finding

that a chaos of facts is the expression of a single underlying fact is like the relief of the musician at resolving a confused mass of sound into melodic and harmonic order. The simplified result is handled with far less mental effort than the original data. The passion for parsimony, for economy of means in thought, is the philosophic passion par excellence; and any character or aspect of the world's phenomena which gathers up their diversity into monotony will gratify that passion ... The knowledge of things by their causes, which is often given as a definition of rational knowledge, is useless unless the causes converge to a minimum number, while still producing the maximum number of effects.

I propose this as the first practical requisite which a philosophic conception must satisfy: It must, in a general way at least, banish uncertainty from the future. I mean the relation of a thing to its future consequences. So long as an object is unusual, our expectations are baffled; they are fully determined as soon as it becomes familiar ... Let now this haunting sense of futurity be thrown off its bearings or left without an object, and immediately uneasiness takes possession of the mind. But in every novel or unclassified experience this is just what occurs; we do not know what will come next; and novelty per se becomes a mental irritant, while custom per se is a mental sedative, merely because the one baffles while the other settles our expectations.'

The three Ps – A summary (Chapters 5 and 6)

(Chapter 5)

1. Prepare = homework and identification (Q × 2) of leads

2. Prospect = attack – on the telephone
– PLANNING
– SCRIPT and CLOSING

1 Greet, identify and ask a simple, factual 'Yes/No' question. PAUSE
2 Get prospect to speak/answer; immediately continue as planned
3 Gain interest – briefly, explain features and the personal benefit of your service offer
4 Establish best time to meet
5 Make appointment. SLOW
6 Confirm appointment

– OBJECTIONS

Happy with/Using competition	Fine. They're a good company, I know of them. I'd simply like to meet you to show you our new services, so that in future you'll have a broader choice of/be in a better position to evaluate between agencies . . . so would . . . OR Fine. They're a good company, I know of them. But I'm sure you'll agree that in such a fast-moving business as ours, it is always valuable to be up to date with what is on offer, and that's why I would like to meet you . . . so would . . .
Too expensive	I take your point Mr/Ms . . . but there have been some changes recently in our pricing structure and I think when we meet you'll appreciate how cost competitive our services now are . . . so would . . .
Used before and found unsatisfactory	I'm sorry to hear that Mr . . . but I believe our new services like . . . would be of great interest to you. They've been very successful for others in your sector and that's why I'd like to come and show you how . . . so would . . .
Not in the market at present/No budget left	I appreciate that Mr . . ., it would have been fortunate indeed if I'd phoned just when you were on the point of commissioning. But there are several new aspects of our service which I believe could be of benefit to you in the future, and that's what I'd like to tell you about when we meet . . . so would . . .
You're too big and sophisticated; we're small	I hear what you say Mr . . ., but I suggest that a meeting would enable us to work out how we could tailor our new service to fit your particular requirements . . . so would . . .

Tell me more now/ Put something in the post	As you can imagine Mr . . . our services are customized so I would need to know more of your particular needs and that can best be done when we meet . . . so would . . .
Too busy	I understand that Mr . . . that's why I'm telephoning for an appointment some time ahead. Let's fix a time for when you're less busy . . . so would . . .
Not interested	I wouldn't expect you to be interested in something new that you haven't had a chance of learning about. I'll have a chance to put that right when we meet . . . so would . . .
I'll think about it	Certainly Mr . . ., but do remember you're under no obligation, so I think you'll be in the best position to make up your mind after we meet . . . so would . . .

More on prospection (Chapter 5)

1 Telephone rules of speech – slow; enthuse; don't interrupt
2 Timing – early or late in the day
3 Have your entire script on ONE page in front of you
4 The secretary – try a range of techniques to get past
5 Log your results – use record sheet
6 Overcoming voicemail – try the long script approach
7 Who are you? – inflate your title
8 Filling your diary – allow for postponements
9 Be prepared for pleasant surprises – keep listening for 'buy' signals
10 Don't worry about personnel changes – go for the new incumbent
11 Allow yourself no excuses – 'just do it'
12 Ride out disappointment – move straight on to the next prospect

3. Present = sell – face to face (Chapter 6)

The cold canvass credentials presentation.

1 The visit – two representatives better than one
2 Equipment – 35mm or laptop
3 The art of listening – dialogue not monologue
4 Sell the benefit NOT the features – '. . . and this is what you get'
5 'Consultative selling' – open; determine needs; present; close
6 Closing the presentation – don't expect an immediate sale
7 The follow up – you have two months to anonymity

The new business pitch against a brief (beauty parade)

'Say what you're going to say; Say it; Say what you've said'

Communication is 58 per cent body – 27 per cent voice – 15 per cent content

Chapter 7

PR

Pr for purpose
Reaching decision-makers

Well-constructed communications plan
Insight into target media
Nominate someone to have the remit for PR
Stories that will interest the media

Basic knowledge of the tools of the trade
Insight into what generates coverage
Zest!

PR stands for press relations as well as public relations (see item 16, Chapter 3). Public relations can help win new business, both directly and indirectly, and this chapter will show you how to use it to provide prospection leads and smooth the way for your cold canvass presentation. Your aim is to tantalize your 'public' into following up on your PR stories and so revealing themselves as prospection targets. Press relations are the means to achieving this end result. I shall utilize the above mnemonic as a guide to the Nine Golden Rules that need to be followed for a successful new business programme using PR.

I PR for purpose

PR may be used for a number of purposes but in the context of this book there is one clear objective, namely the gaining of new business leads. This should be clearly stated from the outset and all in your organization should sign on to it.

Based on lecture material from Claire Spencer, director of planning, Manning Selvage and Lee PR

The object is actively to get your target 'public' to contact you as a result of PR-led actions, and not simply to 'raise awareness'. PR can generate leads and indeed is at its most potent when required to do this. The PR activities in support of the new business drive should be focused on the target 'public' within those industry sectors which are also the aim of that drive; and should feature those very aspects of your offer which will be the key selling focus; in this way you ensure that all is in harmony. And if you want to be contacted you must keep your focus on always, always, always supplying a contact name and phone number as an integral part of your actions. While you cannot force the media to feature them, you have to try. Keep your organization's name consistent across your releases and ensure all your colleagues do so, e.g. decide whether it should be in full or initials? In my own case, is it to be 'Research International', Research International Ltd', or 'RI'?

Of course, PR will generally also create an 'atmosphere', lubrication, within which other new business activities can flourish and often germinate, i.e. PR softens the sell. This work often goes unrecognized.

2 Reaching decision-makers

A target 'public' is defined as those who are specifiers for your product or service. They should be defined in terms of:

● job title
● industry sector
● size of company

If there is any doubt regarding the exact location of decision making for your sector, then preliminary research should clarify the issue. This research can also be used to develop a better understanding of what drives and motivates these decision-makers. If the target audience is not a homogeneous group then it should be prioritized into primary and secondary decision-makers.

3 Well-constructed communications plan

Construct a communications plan that sets out realistic objectives and a strategy to achieve them given any awareness and/or attitude barriers that may exist. It is essential that the whole company, and not just the board, is in agreement with this plan.

Should there be even a degree of uncertainty or disagreement within the company on the current situation regarding outside perceptions, then research should be done among existing and potential clients (possibly lapsed ones also). In addition, an audit should be conducted among primary media to gauge levels of awareness and attitudes to the company.

4 Insight into target media

First identify the channels of media communication, which are likely to fall into the following categories:

- immediate trade titles
- vertical trade titles
- business titles
- national newspapers

From a source such as *PIMS* or *Editors* draw up a list of media and media people (check how up to date they are). You should then be able to have identified the relevant editorial column, editor or journalist for each magazine of interest. Read them all to make up your own mind on how 'PR-able' they are. Then gain supporting data by requesting media packs from the publishing house advertising departments.

5 Nominate someone to have the remit for PR

A PR programme is best managed by a single person. That person will need to demonstrate the following qualifications/experience:

- understanding of new business plan and objectives
- a willingness to badger internally for information
- ability to get people enthused about PR so as to generate story ideas
- confidence to handle sensitive and difficult areas with the media (so make sure your switchboard is instructed to direct all media enquiries to this person)

The PR remit should encompass the development, implementation and evaluation of the PR programme, the co-ordination of all communications with the media, and ensuring any media material featuring client-specific work is approved by the client involved. Ideally the PR programme should be executed on a rolling yearly basis.

6 Stories that will interest the media

- Research/survey based, either:
  - on behalf of an external client
  - bespoke for PR purposes
- Report based, for example:
  - on an industry or market on which the company has a particular view and which could be targeted for new business
  - on trends

- Compelling stories on, for example:
  - a marketing success
  - a human interest story
- Client-generated stories (a big name always interests the media):
  - a new business win (especially if the value can be quantified)
  - how your service/sector got the results
- News:
  - new appointments
  - industry gossip
  - diary snippets

If possible, do not give everything away in your first use of your material. Ideally, your aim should be to tease and tempt, thus generating the need for recipients to contact you when they want to know more. Combined with your focused effort to get the media to feature company name, contact person and telephone number, this should ensure that PR produces lead generation. So, whatever your story, try to hold something back – 'this is just a summary of key points to emerge from our report on client dissatisfaction within the XYZ sector; further data available free from ... on telephone ...'

7 Basic knowledge of the tools of the trade

Media relations go beyond the ubiquitous press release! While the latter remains in your armoury ('... new research from ...'; '... has just been appointed ...'; '... has just hired ...') it is quite distinct from:

- Features, of which there are two types: scheduled and speculative. The scheduled are generally planned by publications between one and three months in advance and it is not difficult to find out which journalist is writing (often a freelancer). He or she can then be approached and will often be receptive to ideas or angles. Speculative features have to be sold in hard and the chance of success is not high, but worth a crack if you have a really good idea.

Journalist briefings are a good idea if the company is less well known. Provide a media pack detailing (in brief) the company, services, key personnel, expertise, client list and case histories. Even here, to gain a first meeting it is advisable to have a 'carrot'.

- Profile your company or a personality within it. This requires some achievement to be recognized in either category, i.e. a success story or an achiever.
- Other possibilities to consider are:
  - opinion platforms, such as a controversial opinion on an industry issue
  - a diary piece, if funny, quirky
  - letters: spontaneous or reacting to something written by others – be controversial (if you can back it up!).

8 Insight into what generates coverage

Do not be despondent if coverage is not generated immediately. There are a number of factors that may influence whether or not coverage is likely to appear:

- pressure of space; pre-empted by a bigger story – bad luck but you could try again on another date
- lack of familiarity with your company among the media
- trust in your company and the information supplied
- timing: did the information reach the title in time?
- relevance to title: is it tailored or is it too obviously an 'omnibus' release?
- strength of story – big name, big bucks, supported by statistics?
- pre-emptive coverage in another title
- satiation with the story by the media
- sell in was 'laboured'
- caught the journalist on press day; this cannot be emphasized enough – get your timing right by doing some homework on deadlines

9 Zest

Always be alert to opportunities. These may be created by events (political, social, or economic); by editorial comment; by industry issues or by developments in the company. Be aware of opportunities beyond the media; by speaker platforms, seminar convening, and sponsorship openings.

What about hearing from an actual journalist? Here are the comments of the editor of the *Yorkshire Post* (as quoted in *Professional Marketing*, November 1997). He states that coverage in the press requires 'stories with an angle':

- timing is crucial with news – don't send details of a deal a week after completion
  always look for an interesting angle or unusual feature to position the story
- resonance with the readership is important – find out who you are talking to and do so in terms they will understand
- use the 'Pub Test' – is the story something you would talk about in the pub?
- an interesting, unusual or quirky photograph is often the key to success in placing a news item
- above all it's about people
- have supporting material to hand which can be supplied by fax or e-mail immediately
- be prepared to answer questions 'off the back' of press releases

Fictional case study
– or how not to do it!

From Claire Spencer

Wier, Fuller, Bull

We have here a large, successful sales promotion company run by its three partners: Wier being responsible for print and sourcing, Fuller acting as creative director, and Bull as chairman. They have enjoyed steady growth and have a blue-chip client base. They have achieved some fame for their organization already through their giant plastic roses promotion and their singing mugs. But this is all in the past.

At the moment we meet them, all is not rosy – new business has been poor and there is a feeling that their profile is flagging. At a board meeting they discussed what they should do, particularly with respect to PR. It emerged that they all had different objectives: Wier believed that he was an industry wiz at sourcing new ideas and was at that moment exclusively sourcing an innovatory singing pencil from Taiwan which he wanted to feature in the trade press. Fuller's agenda was self-serving; she wanted to see her name up in lights because she was intending to set up on her own in the near future. Bull was totally financially motivated – he wasn't particularly interested in sales promotion but was looking for an opportunity to sell the company to the highest bidder. (Others attending the board included the financial director, who didn't relish the expense of PR, and the new business director, who was desperate for any help to save his job.)

With so many disparate agendas it was not surprising that disagreement flourished. This manifested itself again when consideration turned to target groups. Wier was looking at suppliers, Fuller at her peer group, and Bull at the financial markets. Others felt they should be targeting marketing personnel, although even here they could not agree at which level they should be aiming.

Nor did they have much of an idea as to what their current image might be among any of these potential targets. And indeed if they did have such an idea it was usually quite wrong. While they thought of themselves as old hands in the industry, their image was in fact one of 'wide boys'. Strategy was in no way seen as their strong point, and many had grasped the real motivation that underlay Bull's actions. Relations with the media had faded away leaving no real close contacts who could inform them of the situation.

Not surprisingly, they could not agree on who should mastermind the PR campaign on which they were now to embark. It became everybody's responsibility! Yet nobody knew who was talking to whom. With the inevitable result that journalists received a release from two different people simultaneously on the same subject. Then a vital release went out without client approval – particularly crucial when the promotion featured the queen on a mug that played the national anthem!!

Quite simply – Wier, Fuller, Bull – was a name that suited them perfectly! Their purpose was unclear, their target unfocused, their plan non-existent, and their insight faulty. Under these circumstances PR cannot flourish.

Chapter 8

Advertising

'It is far easier to write ten passably effective sonnets, good enough to take in the not too enquiring critic, than one effective advertisement that will take in a few thousand of the uncritical buying public.'

Aldous Huxley

Beyond the anticipated awareness and image-building benefits that the exceptional advertisement can achieve, I am more interested in whether advertising can generate leads? Or does it spread the net too thin and wide? In fact, do you need it at all? Given the limited numbers of prospects who buy in the professional services arena and the infrequency of their purchase decision making, a coherent case needs to be made before doing any advertising. Why do so few ad agencies advertise? There must be a message in that!

Of course, for many years, some professional services were not permitted to advertise for so-called ethical reasons. When these restrictions were lifted the first impulse was to imitate their fmcg cousins and rush into advertising. They were unaware that fmcg had moved on and below-the-line activity had overtaken above the line.

My own interest in advertising for professional services is in its role as a response generator (see the first example at the end of the chapter). But the desire to become famous, to be talked about remains a strong one and is often hard to resist – despite the likelihood that most advertising in the professional sphere will leave your prospects cold and tends to succeed rather in getting competition rattled – which may be satisfying enough! Your colleagues will always be seduced by the opportunity to mount an ad campaign. It is your job to focus their attention on the additional benefit it can offer to lead generation.

There is one obvious circumstance in which the use of advertising can be defended with ease – the launch of a new professional services agency or a new service offer. Announcement advertising aimed at building awareness has a valuable role to prepare the ground for all the other activities detailed in this book. If the benefit is truly new and if the advertising is produced with real flair and creativity, then its impact can be quite dramatic, generating spontaneous enquiries and creating a buzz within the industry. So, more than ever, do not forget to put a response mechanism on the ad to allow reactions to get straight back to you.

There is also a similar role for advertising when a new business campaign is being instigated for an existing agency or service. A number of the Twenty Golden Rules enunciated in Chapter 3 imply some function for advertising: namely, taking a long-term view; the agency as a brand; creating a marketing strategy. A well thought out media plan for a well-planned and executed advertising campaign can underpin the entire strategy, ease the path for the other elements of the marketing mix, and maintain a steady trickle of new leads.

Although unquantifiable, who can deny the lubrication of curiosity that advertising may create, which then smoothes the way for the prospecting call or the direct response mail shot? Not forgetting the effect inside your own organization, where the advertising acts as proof of commitment to the marketing initiative and raises morale (the reinforcement role).

Yet what are most professional services advertisements like? Study the print media and you will find . . . they're all very similar for a start. And of poor average quality.

- Tombstones! – black and white, obituary-style, death rather than life
- Boring! – offering nothing new, nothing enticing
- Over scripted! – reams and reams of illegible small print
- Pompous! – 'the leader in . . .', '. . . we're No. 1'
- Feature rather than benefit driven! – 'we do this', 'we offer that' rather than 'we can help you for this', 'we can do that for you better, quicker, and cheaper than others can'
- The curse of the metaphor! – the headline or visual which could apply to any company in your sector (the headline 'scoop the pool with us'; the visual of jigsaw pieces – 'we put it all together for you'; the staircase visual – 'let us help you get to the top')

Would many or any of these really contribute to a sophisticated buyer of professional services changing his or her decision to appoint new or stick to their current advisors? Surely we can agree that our clients buy people and yet none of the professional service suppliers seem willing to attempt the difficult task of getting that personal chemistry over via an advertisement.

Only Andersen Consulting have, to my knowledge, taken their message to the highest level within the mass media and gone on television with brilliant, professional executions appealing to both the emotions and the rational. A few others have utilized the economies of radio. For the majority of us, print is the only possible, affordable medium (and usually fixed at a maximum of a single page in colour).

Advertising theories come and go, but the basic starting point, however old fashioned it may seem, remains the USP. As a minimum, there must be a USP – a Unique Selling Proposition – comprising a benefit that is uniquely yours and which attracts. Then you must gain attention. Two classical quotes made many years ago from the boss of US ad agency Ted Bates, Rosser Reeves, relate to the power of this key pair of factors in advertising –

> 'Once you've found a USP any good copywriter can write a good ad. The rest is just wordsmithing. Not that wordsmithing isn't important – we pay a fortune for copywriting talent. But five top copywriters might turn out five entirely different ads, all good, from a single USP – while all the wordsmithing in the world won't move the product if the claim isn't right'

> 'A farmer had wanted to buy a superior mule all his life. He saved his money, and paid thousands of dollars for a mule – but he got a stubborn one. When he got it into the barn it wouldn't move. So he chained it to the tractor and dragged it ten miles down the road to a mule trainer. The mule trainer said he would train the mule, and the farmer asked him how much.
>
> "Five dollars" was the reply.
>
> "That's a reasonable price," said the farmer. "Go ahead."
>
> The mule trainer dragged the mule into his barn, picked up a 45 pound sledgehammer and hit the mule right between the eyes. The mule went "oof."
>
> "For God's sake," cried the farmer. "I hired you to train him not to kill him!"
>
> "Sure, I'll train him. But first," said the mule trainer, "first I've got to get his attention."'

Creating a print ad with both a USP and impact is a skill, which, taken with the broad visibility of the end product, demands the hiring in of professionals to execute it effectively – a good idea from the chairman sketched on a napkin after a business lunch is not normally a good idea at all. There must be no economizing here, no DIY – although the possibility of using contra-deals has already been mentioned; nor should the availability of freelancers be forgotten (many of them would die for an opportunity to show their capabilities in front of a 'trade' audience). But set a clear budget and give a clear brief.

If you make your advertising professional you will easily stand out from the crowd. At the risk of repetition, please, please do not forget the response mechanism – one of your aims still remains to sell a meeting, so give the target the chance to identify him or herself so that you can follow up and prospect for that meeting. All ads should carry a specific and senior contact name alongside your organization's contact numbers, encouraging a response. As all direct, off-the-page sales organizations have known for years, direct response of this type allows a quick means of gauging the relative success of different executions. Make sure that all staff who take incoming calls check the source of any potential client's enquiry to aid this evaluation of the effectiveness of above-the-line advertising.

When purchasing advertising space there is one key word – negotiate! Few pay quoted page rates, so nor should you. Go for the special offer, which may mean waiting until the last moment; but think twice about the special supplement, which is usually just an advertising vehicle where you will find yourself surrounded by all your competitors, thus reducing your impact. Fight to get colour for no extra cost; to gain a full page for the price of a half; demand a repeat at a token extra price! You want to be run of the page, in with the news and out on your own. Of course the space salesperson you will be dealing with has probably been indoctrinated with just those telesales techniques outlined in this book – so use your inside knowledge to resist the blandishments, and stick to your guns.

And don't forget trade directories and *Yellow Pages* (see second example below). In these cases, beware the space salespeople that approach not only you but many of your fellow partners/directors, aiming to achieve a sale with at least one of them. You may suddenly find that you are in a multiplicity of directories, each at a reasonable price, each with a justifiable niche, but adding up to a total spend that is way beyond your budget. Ensure that there is only a single person who has responsibility for sign-off and control of the ad spend.

Then there is the Internet! Everybody's doing it – but results are unclear. You can't resist the tide, but at least you can do something different. Remember the credo – 'be helpful' – and that means offering interest and/or value – a web site that offers data, or offers training/instruction, or a game. In return, you may gain the one and only thing you are really looking for – that the visitor identifies him or herself so you can follow up! I sympathize with this overview of web marketing developments from Philippe Boutie (*ESOMAR Newsbrief*):

Yesterday – the first era of Internet Marketing
This was the Web Brochure era. If you were on the web you were cool. Just showing your brand or company there and immersing it in hip graphic design was enough. Pretty soon, every brand or company had its marketing site. And they all suffered from the same syndrome – the ABOUT US syndrome. Their sites all looked the same.

Today – the second era of Internet Marketing

Providing something of value to their site visitors. About YOU, not about US. These sites build traffic and relationships by giving the visitor access to information. The expected pay-off is that a satisfied visitor will move on to the 'about us' section. This is state-of-the-art today.

Tomorrow – the third era of Internet Marketing

The main purpose now is to crystallize the company's personality – to provide a rich interactive experience, to make the company become an old friend before you've even met it. Stylistic effects are not self-indulgence, but on image and emotion.

What about sponsorship? I personally must confess to having no experience of its use. It certainly seems increasingly relevant, though rather for awareness building or maintenance than to convey anything but the briefest of messages. Synergy with your clients' profiles and with your own image would seem to be the judgement criteria for selecting the right sponsorship vehicle – sport, conference, book, charity, seminar, award, etc. The same applies to celebrity endorsement – look for the synergy.

You should approach sponsorship exactly as you would any other marketing activity – set out your targets, shortlist your options, prepare a full proposal, agree criteria for success.

In conclusion, my advice is – you do not have to advertise/go on the Internet/sponsor. Only do it if it has a real, justifiable place in your marketing strategy. And only do it if you can do it well.

Two case studies on advertising

I am indebted to Tom Rayfield, now retired from JWT Advertising, for these two humorous but true examples of (1) the value of a response mechanism, and (2) the simple rules of advertising to a budget.

Advertising 1 – Example of response mechanisms

When I joined the agency I was immediately put onto the account of a hearing aid company, which I suppose is a service industry since it didn't actually make anything, except a lot of money. It had small billings and took lots of small solus ads on the front pages of any newspaper likely to be read by deaf old people! – probably the *Telegraph*!

My ad, composed only three days after joining the agency, was as follows: 'Breakthrough in Hearing. New American aid needs nothing in either ear'. (And probably not much between them either as far as customers were concerned!) The body copy continued with descriptive phrases such as 'years of dedicated research', 'unique tympano technique', 'only available from us', and 'free hearing test record'.

I knew nothing about advertising, but had applied some commonsense rules:

- Identify the target audience's problem big and bold – deafness
- Promise them something new and helpful immediately – an aid
- Sell as hard as possible – only from us
- Offer a relevant incentive – free test record

The ad ran for six years unchanged because the enquiries flowed in and the cost per reply was only 25p.

Advertising 2 – Example of using a limited budget

Imagine you're a local plumber in the country – a service company, with maybe £5000 a year to spend on advertising. You are probably tempted to advertise in the local freesheet (because it's cheaper than the local newspaper) and in the church magazine. Neither of these are the most effective way to spend your little budget. The need for a plumber is occasional, so surely the best and most important place you need to advertise is in *Yellow Pages*.

But that's where any other intelligent local plumber will also be advertising. So how do you make potential customers phone you and not them?

All you have to do is ask yourself two simple questions. The answers are more difficult than the questions – why should anyone flicking through the 'plumber' section phone me? What do I offer that no one else does?

The answer may (and probably should be) functional – 'we guarantee to have a man round within sixty minutes because we're your local plumber; and if we don't make it we'll do the job free'. But it may be non-functional – 'all our plumbers wear a clean uniform, so you'll recognize them'.

Then there is only one thing left to do. Make sure your phone number is big enough to be read easily by a distressed caller surrounded by floods. A check of the local *Yellow Pages* will show that almost no one is doing these two simple things, regardless of the size of their ad.

Chapter 9

Direct marketing

Direct marketing is *not* direct mail. Direct marketing is a marketing method and direct mail is just one of the media available. It traditionally formed a large part of direct marketing – and is still about half – but it is being overtaken gradually by the increasing number of press and TV ads with some response device. So the importance of direct marketing, and the aspect of it that is most relevant to the credo of this book, is once again this response device. It forms a part of 'pull' marketing, as defined in Chapter 4. The objective is to entice the prospect to emerge from the darkness and respond, thereby identifying him or her, on the basis of which you can begin your prospection and cold canvass activities. Such a response device should always feature on advertising (or could itself be the core of that advertisement); it certainly must be an integral part of any direct mail you use.

In all cases your objective is to hear from your prospective client, hoping that this will start a conversation, maybe permit an appointment, and lead to a real problem-solving discussion, a first job and eventually a business relationship. And don't forget existing clients – if you've got something new to say, then they should hear about it first – they are the most fertile ground for any messages you may wish to send, offering the potential for increased and cross selling. Nor should you omit consideration of the telephone as a means of making your offer, of setting up the 'bait', and generating interest – nothing is more 'direct'.

This chapter will not advocate telephone sales or mass mailings. The first of these is irrelevant to professional services marketing where personal contact is the objective (and the crucial role of the telephone for prospecting has already been dealt with); the second is relevant, but only where there is a really universal offer – see the next chapter for using print material in this way and remember the HELPLINE idea (Chapter 4 case study: a classic response mechanism with a clear user benefit). There are agencies, consultants and books enough telling you how to do mass mailings.

Based on lecture material from Tom Rayfield, ex-JWT

My interest is in identifying target prospects, and for this the response device is crucial – whatever the carrier vehicle. I want you to do direct marketing –

When you have a specific offer . . .

. . . for which clients and prospects need to contact you

I don't say that it should be as crude as 'Buy now while stocks last!' or 'Purchase one, get one free!' But the underlying idea is the same, targeted only at those with the relevant need, and linked back to a named individual in your organization, plus phone or fax number.

Having developed such an offer, with a clear benefit aimed at a specific target group, which you may now indeed wish to publicize through the mail (and in some cases you may exceptionally be called upon to do a mass mailing) you **must** always use a response mechanism. Put yourself in the position of the receivers of your offer message – 'How can I get hold of this?' – and make it easy for them. In addition, you can at least try to avoid simple errors that may negate the positive result you wish to achieve from your mailing. Learn from the experiences of someone on the receiving end of such actions; in this case a direct marketer himself (Tom Rayfield) who decided to become his own laboratory rat (as described in his two publications *Dear Personalised* and *Dear Sir or Madam*, available from JWT.) Having monitored his own mail both at home and in the office, and his attempts to respond, he was able to reveal some horror stories of direct marketing gone wrong and also to draw some useful conclusions:

> 'My household gets over 500 mailshots a year. Last year a building society sent to our house a very elaborate mailshot about a really clever pension plan they had devised which would unlock all the money you might have hidden away in previous employers' pension schemes and put it into one great heap. It was addressed to my 17-year-old son! He has indeed got an account with them and they know how old he is, because he got their Junior Savers kit a few years ago. But they have blown any kind of trust he might have in them knowing and caring about him.'

> 'At work, I get at least as many mailshots as at home. It is patently obvious from the offers I am made that at least half of them have no idea at all about what my company does. I responded to one company – two weeks later I got their brochure.'

Tom reminds us that if we are mailing out, we must remember . . .

● There is no such thing as 'junk' mail – only mail that is badly targeted and misdirected. All mail has the opportunity to be impactful and interesting – it's your job to make it so. Even to bin it requires an effort from the recipient, and in that short moment of truth lies your opportunity.

- The competitive context: your prospect probably receives 100 lbs of unsolicited material per annum comprising over 500 items. Ask yourself why your mailshot should be treated any different from the rest, i.e. go straight into the bin!
- If you send ten items of literature to perfect strangers, two of them will be binned unopened, another two will be opened but not read. What a waste of expensive print material. OK six will be read. But how many get acted upon depends on the items listed below. (Note: this situation is even worse when you are writing to businesses since there is the additional secretarial filter factor.)
- About one-third of mailshots are wrongly addressed – so ask yourself why yours should be any better? Only if you work on it.
- Try not to look too obviously like junk mail; consider all possibilities for personalization – the handwritten envelope, the use of a Christian name, using a stamp rather than franking, etc.
- Get the timing right: in advance of known seasonal activities, allowing sufficient time to get into diaries, just before budgets are being set, etc.
- Get the language right; good English, no mistakes, brief and to the point, the offer clear and unambiguous (maybe repeated), etc.
- Even if you don't have much money, at least have a good idea; so try to be interesting, relevant, and original – helpful too.

When you are trying to generate a response, remember that there is no 'ideal' per cent response rate – just the profit per reply calculation. Tom again:

'Traditional wisdom says that to be successful you must get a 2 per cent response rate to your mailings. This is nonsense. All you need to know is the profit per reply. We spent £300 000 for one client and got just 150 responses. But each of them was interested in renting a building which implied an expenditure with our client of £6 million a year'

But that profit is only available to you if you react promptly to the requests that come in. So . . .

- Make sure you get back to each response quickly – ideally within hours, certainly within days.
  If you follow up with postal material, make sure your company name is on the outside – they've sent for it and will be looking out for it (you don't want it binned with other junk mail).
- Whatever you send or however you follow up, make sure it's relevant and interesting. Also, it must be clearly stated (or clear in your mind) what the next step will be.

Don't forget to reply to any such activities generated by your competitors – if you don't know what they're doing how will you know what to offer yourselves? If they are cocky or stupid enough to make an offer to all and sundry, why not take advantage of it yourself? Get their material and analyse it in your own terms – what does it tell you about their own strategy, about their service focus, about their targeting, etc?

To recap, as with advertising, approach direct marketing by:

● Stating the target audience's problem
  – the best headline or opening sentence states a problem that you can be almost certain your reader can personally empathize with ...
● Promising a solution
  ... and then you proceed to provide the solution in your body copy; a solution that only you can solve (or at which you excel)
● Asking for a response
  – don't waste time, don't vacillate – sell hard

Before any of the above can be effective you face what is probably the biggest hurdle – your own database/mailing list. Let me repeat the whole of Chapter 3, Item 10 – and please believe it.

10 Treasure your database

This is absolutely vital in order to track prospects (and indeed your clients.) It is amazing how few companies have a good database and, even if they do, how poorly they use it (very often its use does not extend beyond the Christmas cards!). It should be a repository for information on each client and provide the basis for a regular and meaningful contact with them, i.e. the heart of a communications strategy.

I am not the person to recommend the ideal software to you. The offer is enormous, experience varied, evidence of good practice almost negligible. No one is happy. But one thing I can suggest is – don't be too ambitious. Size is not everything! It's what you do with it that's the key. It's much better to have a small active database than an enormous macho one that lies unused and unloved. Because a good database requires a major effort just to build it and then constant tending to maintain it – it is always out of date. Who's going to do this? It makes one hell of a difference to the resource required for this whether you are dealing with hundreds or many thousands of records.

But the last thing you want to do is to starve your database of the information it requires to be effective. Keep reminding your staff (and yourself) to enter updates on existing clients monthly. After every new business prospection call, every meeting, every pitch, there must be a contact report and information added to the existing record or a new one set up. It is never-ending. It is a responsibility that should not be delegated. It is too easy to pass the task on to an office junior who will, through no fault of his or her own, simply validate the familiar maxim of 'garbage in, garbage out'. Only those directly in contact with clients or prospects can have any chance of confirming the data is correct, spotting spelling mistakes, remembering that article in the trade press announcing the company that has moved office or the client that has moved company.

Custom made or off the shelf? Current software developments allow almost anyone to build their own database very easily nowadays. But the advice again must be to consider the use of a professional list in addition. There are many purchasable databases around. They are not perfect (assume 15 per cent is going to be out of date before it even reaches you) but they offer you the opportunity to spend your time going out and making contacts rather than being stuck on the telephone laboriously trying to identify each contact from your own list of companies. If you buy, don't be seduced by numbers: buy no more than you can keep up to date.

Finally, protect your database. It's valuable and horribly mobile. So back it up all the time and lock it (physically and via passwords). To lose so much effort would really be a crime, in more than one sense.

Force your colleagues (and yourself) to check the listings monthly and amend, add and junk. It's deadly boring but has to be done. Remember – junk mail is simply mail that is poorly or wrongly targeted. A good time to do a mailing is soon after Christmas – because most of your people only get round to cleaning the database for the Christmas card list! In January, the list is still relatively fresh; it decays as the year goes on.

A further checklist for direct mail (courtesy of Simon Rhind-Tutt):

- Have something new to say – otherwise why bother
- Show you understand their business – you want to be helpful
- Keep it simple – if you cannot make an offer that is capable of being understood by the secretary, ask yourself why
- Be relevant – stick to a single message
- Put it all on one page – it must be possible
- Sign it yourself – personalization is still an advantage in today's mass world
- Handwrite the envelopes, if possible (see above for reasoning)
- Don't be afraid to test – a small-scale pilot distribution with the response logged and some follow-up interviews
- Honour the promise of a follow-up call – if you say you will, then you must do it
- Double check for typos
- BE PROVOCATIVE – to gain attention, not to antagonize
- BE INTERESTING – no more 'me-too', please

I've said you must demand a response, both for its intrinsic value and also in order to be able to follow up via cold canvass. Can you handle these responses? They could be of considerable volume and all coming in during a brief time period following your mailing. This issue has already been raised in this chapter, i.e. are the phones manned during the times specified, are the follow-up materials available and in sufficient quantities, are respondents' details comprehensively logged, etc. Tom Rayfield analysed his own attempts to respond to direct marketing offers and found that only 60 per cent of those organizations he tested responded within seven days (and 20 per cent took more than twenty-seven days or did not reply at all).

You may feel you are well-equipped – I hope that you will agree that it is worth checking out objectively whether you really are. The major service organizations, the Post Office, banks, retail outlets, who are vitally dependent on delivering excellent service ('Delighting the Customer' as it is often called), spend vast amounts of money testing/auditing their own service delivery standards and benchmarking them against their main competitors. It is called service or business control monitoring and the exercise to evaluate it usually goes under the title of mystery customer research, or mystery shopping. Outsiders are recruited to play the role of customers of the service under investigation, and they log their experiences in considerable detail – e.g. how rapidly is the phone answered? How knowledgeable are the staff? How quickly are materials despatched upon request? Are the right answers given to queries? How friendly are contact personnel? etc.

You should assess your own response systems in this manner, too. At least you could make a start on a small scale by using friends or family (with the relevant profile) to act the part of your customers. At best, you should hire an outside consultant to do it.

An additional useful feature is to plan in advance a series of scenarios for these mystery shoppers to act out. These are designed to test out specific aspects of your systems, e.g. they can play the role of the difficult prospect ('I urgently need to receive your brochure by tomorrow'), the questioning caller ('Who exactly in your organization should I address my enquiry for XYZ to?'), you can test out response to a female as opposed to a male caller, record speed in answering the call and the functioning of internal transfers or voicemail messaging, and so on.

The results should be disseminated across the organization. But do warn your people in advance that this audit is happening, otherwise you will be accused of spying. Indeed the warning itself should act as a powerful stimulus for your staff to be constantly on the alert, never knowing if a caller is real or a mystery!

Chapter 10

Print material

Earlier chapters have made clear my own views on this topic. In particular, the frequently seen obsession with the company brochure has been, and must again be, put under the cold light of scrutiny.

Yes, of course you need a company brochure. It will often be requested by outsiders and often be left behind by your staff as a calling card. Your own staff, new recruits, and potential staff will all expect you to have one – and may indeed be the most avid readers of it.

But it is unlikely to be the means to winning new business. I doubt that potential clients are going to make their selection of provider based on it, and I suspect they will have a low probability of reading it. They will treat it as a calling card at best (filing it for reference) and as junk at worst.

And this is despite months, if not years, of brochure gestation within your organization: a birth process that often produces intense passions and deep-seated company rifts – either because it represents the MD's ego trip, or as a result of a committee process that produces the three-humped camel. Not forgetting the expense – of hours in discussion and argument, of money for high quality print, presentation, and quantity.

When the boxes of brochures in their thousands finally arrive a question comes along with them: 'what do we do now?' It transpires that no attention was paid to this matter during the development period, so focused was everyone on the content rather than on application.

The answer usually given has a predictable logic: 'well, there's no point in having them gather dust here – send them out.' So these expensive documents are mass mailed to all and sundry; and guess what – nothing happens! No thank-you letters, no congratulatory notes, no new business opportunities.

Because brochures are not sales vehicles. They tend to be full of 'we' and 'me' phraseology, to comprise lists and lists of 'what we can do', and to be technique and feature oriented and not related at all to the 'help' motif or benefit that has underpinned everything recommended in this book.

Here is a funny/sad but real example of an incredible extreme of listing, taken from *Private Eye* and credited to a doctor's brochure seen in South Africa:

> You will pay attention!! Doctor Ngunga is here to solve all your economic as well as social problems. He can also tell you all your problems before you say anything to him. He can treat more than 48 diseases at a reasonable price. Examples of diseases/problems are listed below:
>
> 1) insanity 2) diarrhoea 3) bewitched people 4) one with bad luck 5) men's penis which cannot erect powerfully 6) women with pregnancy problems 7) vomiting all the time 8) asthma 9) woman who cannot produce 10) gonorrhoea 11) lack of strength in the body 12) to be liked at work 13) bad smelling breath and also prevent thieves from attacking homes 14) education 15) promotion 16) pressure 17) diabetes 18) customers attraction 19) court cases 20) tuberculosis 21) demand debts 22) removal of misunderstandings with anybody
>
> Don't hesitate to pay him a visit. You are most welcome.

Is your own brochure really so different?

Another relevant quote on this subject –

> QUESTION: What is the most abused or misused marketing tool in your profession?
>
> *Accountants*: Piles and piles of procrastinating glossy brochures that cost a fortune and are read by no one. Few professionals think what they want a brochure for, they just want one. The worst offenders are the ones that talk about philosophy and values when what the client wants to know about are demonstrable benefits. Looking back in my career, I'm sure that I've even seen situations where brochures were really only produced for internal territorial demarcation; not even internal communication, let alone something as clever as targeted direct mail.
>
> *Surveyors*: Brochures – they are seen as the panacea for all marketing problems and opportunities. Too often they are produced without the necessary thought on how they will be used, what they will say and what they hope to achieve.
>
> *Professional Marketing*, April 1993

In fact, the planning and the production of the company brochure should be seen as a necessary starting point in a process aimed at producing a range of print material for the company. Your thinking should be extended to include your corporate ID and general design issues. Once the brochure has been got out of the way, the real creative thinking can start, aimed at producing genuinely client oriented, helpful material that will be 'collectable' rather than 'binable'.

A new approach

What then are the options? Let's consider five: newsletters, monographs, surveys, directories, and advertorials (the Internet, which could be justified as electronic print, has been dealt with previously). The common thread is that they all take an element of your company's expertise and, without giving away the entire secret, put it at the client's disposal – thereby offering genuine help in a convenient format. As a result, it is highly likely that the material will be kept by the recipient and so become a selling tool due to its whetting of the appetite and its longevity.

1 **Newsletters**
   A valuable print tool if well produced. But don't underestimate the time taken to prepare: colleagues who promise material often don't deliver, print deadlines creep up on you, and suddenly you realize that publishing 'only once a quarter' is far from easy. They will not work as a 'hobby'; newsletters have to be taken seriously if you want them to become collectables. They have to be single-mindedly client oriented offering really up-to-date news, controversial opinion pieces, technical advice, etc. They must eschew navel gazing, staff items, ego massage, etc.
      Despatch should be to the widest possible audience of existing and potential clients.

2 **Monographs** (see example on pages 129–30)
   These fit the 'help' motif perfectly, offering views and comment on technical/topical issues. They also tend to have an extremely long shelf life and so do not present such a constant demand for new material as do the newsletters.
      They are referred to in the plural because it is anticipated that there will be a series of monographs, with new ones issued at (unspecified) intervals. Ideally they will have a unique style which, together with the company logo, should make them instantly recognizable. They should also have a clear contact name, address and number for any follow up.
      Distribution needs to be considered carefully. These are likely to be well-produced items. For this reason, and because each monograph deals with one specific issue, they are not suitable for mass mailing, in contrast to newsletters. Targeting is required, and as a result it is recommended that advertising is utilized to inform interested parties of the existence and range of

material on offer and to provide the means for them to identify themselves, i.e. through use of a response mechanism. (Existing clients can be informed through a mailing or indeed an announcement in a newsletter.)

3 **Surveys**

Not a surprising suggestion given that the author is from the market research profession originally. There can be little doubt of the interest that can be aroused from the 'factual authority' of a market research study. Under such titles as 'An industry view . . .' or 'What clients want . . .', great interest and PR value can be achieved from either quantitative (sample of 100+) or qualitative (focus groups or in-depth interviews) studies under your sponsorship. But it behoves the author to warn about costs (not less than thousands of pounds) set against the dubious value of studies that skimp on design and sample size in order to produce headline findings for PR only. A professional should always be consulted to avoid some sharp operator (unlikely to be the press, more likely to come from an intelligent competitor) destroying the validity of the survey and making you look cheap and foolish.

4 **Directories**

A variation on the monograph theme. In this case you are providing some sort of convenient listing which the client can use for reference purposes, e.g. statistics, listings, abstracts, etc. The benefits are those of the monograph, and distribution should follow the same pattern.

5 **Advertorials**

Many trade magazines are willing to produce supplements based on company-produced material. These enhance the value of that issue of the magazine, yet require little or no journalistic input since you will have written most or all of it. Your name will feature prominently as sponsor and free run-ons will offer you further distribution options. So it is a win-win situation for you and the magazine.

Design and corporate identity

Whenever consideration turns to print material, the question of design comes to the fore – current or new? In-house or bought-in? Style? Quality of finish? And the next step often then becomes one of reviewing corporate identity.

Let's be clear – design undoubtedly has a vital role in the presentation and marketing of a professional services organization. It is a key means for you to distinguish yourself from your competition. It is a way to reveal your personality. It is one manner of helping you to differentiate yourself. The same goes for your logo and corporate identity. The mix of ID and house style will feature on all your materials – letters, presentations, fax headers, documents – and so will have a direct bearing on your new business success (with initial impact when you send your appointment confirmation letter to the prospect after the telephone call, and then, vitally, during your credentials presentation and in the materials left behind).

Under such circumstances it is crucial that the initiative for any review of design/corporate ID comes from the very top of your organization and that high quality outside professionals (ideally, with experience in your sector) are brought in to handle the exercise. The need for authority inside and outside your organization is because this operation is almost certain to result in proposals for change, and change is something many resist.

A full and clear brief must be given to the agency selected, which should focus on the personality of your firm that you wish to transmit and the strategic objectives that underlie it. Remember that design works at an emotional as well as a rational level, so address both of them in your brief. Help the designers by providing examples of your competitors' literature and corporate IDs. The designers will almost certainly start with a communications audit of all your current materials. When they return with their proposals, listen to their rationale, be prepared for creative solutions, and take a long-term view in your decision making. Beware of the difficulties of making decisions by committee. Ask the simple question – has the designer identified who you are and stressed your points of difference?

Be prepared to ask questions about the cost of implementation and demand that you gain an understanding of production issues, e.g. use of colours, illustrations, and photography. You should also demand a design or identity manual to ensure strict guidelines are given and adhered to regarding all materials. There is a great temptation for staff to play with the design format, moving logos around the page, adding or removing elements, etc. Having a manual can help to reduce this.

Bear in mind that print and design material will have a long shelf life, so take a long-term view and beware of following fashion trends that can quickly become dated. Keep names of personnel out of the material as far as possible – they are the most susceptible to change!

Introduction

Usage and attitude studies provide the basic building blocks for marketing activity since they are conducted to provide an understanding of the market in which a particular brand is, or is planned, to be sold.

This type of research sets out to provide a description of the market from the consumer's point of view with the objective of identifying market opportunities, optimising brand positioning or identifying target markets.

The scope of the study will be infinitely variable as each study must be designed to meet the needs of the particular market at issue. It may be brand specific or designed to look at product types within a broad market area.

Most usage and attitude studies will, however, examine such issues as:

- Brand/product awareness (including advertising awareness where relevant).

- Brand/product usership – including trial, loyalty, repertoire.

- Brand purchase – frequency, source, prices paid, sizes.

- Brand/product use, frequency, quantity, ways used, by whom etc.

- Attitudes to or beliefs about products or brands – the consumer view of positioning.

- Needs of consumers in the market and what is important to them.

In addition relevant information would be collected to enable all of these to be looked at in terms of the demographic and attitudinal characteristics of the product users, such that the data may be used to segment the market as an aid to the targetting of new products, relaunching existing brands, advertising or other marketing activity.

The opportunity is also frequently taken to look at other issues (such as pricing, packaging, reactions to new concepts, media use, or product ownership in other areas) – which can then be looked at in the context of the behaviour and attitudes in this market.

Usage and attitude studies may be repeated at regular intervals to identify trends in behaviour, or attitudes, and to isolate the characteristics of those sectors which may be expanding or contracting.

Chapter 11

Keeping the customers happy

Assuming that the jobs you have worked on have delivered the promise you originally offered, you will continue to keep clients happy between project briefs the same way that you won them over in the first place – by being helpful. Your aim is for repeat business at the very least, and ideally to expand their business year on year. There are many actions you can and should take to keep the sources of the new business you have won at such effort.

This is not the place to argue the case for the benefits and limitations of BS 5750/ISO 9000 in your organization as a means of ensuring that everything has gone as planned on each project handled so far. Some see quality standards as applicable to procedural matters only and offering no more than a heavy bureaucratic overload of manuals and forms. Others find they serve genuinely to improve quality and act as a safety net and reassurance to clients. Certainly they require complaints logging and regular client satisfaction measurement, which is a valuable discipline, so long as it does not become too onerous and repetitious a task for the respondent.

Even better than the routine of despatching standardized customer satisfaction questionnaires is the infrequent but in-depth client review meeting. This provides the occasion for real, frank discussion from which one can learn much more about one's status within the range of suppliers that they use. Before going into such a meeting there should be an internal review also.

On the agenda here are two key issues – first, a realistic assessment of the monetary value of the client to your organization; second, a review of cross-selling opportunities. In the first case you should be assigning a value to you of the client: everyone instinctively knows that not all clients are profitable and that some are more profitable than others. Get the figures and study them, including a 'lifetime' projection. In the second case, we are talking about you and your colleagues co-operating in order to exploit the opportunities within a client organization to the full. This raises the fraught topic of cross selling. Why fraught? – because it involves internal rivalries in your organization. I can only warn you while fully endorsing these extracts from the words of Ross Fishman (*Professional Marketing*, November 1997). Read on:

> As cross selling goes there are two kinds of professional firms:
>
> 1 Those firms where trust is implicit in the culture, and fee earners co-operate to serve the needs of the clients regardless of the compensation system; and . . .
> 2 Those on planet earth
>
> Some marketers act as though clients have monthly team meetings to uncover opportunities to give the firm more, and more varied, business. Experience shows that it ain't necessarily so. In fact, it ain't remotely so.

He goes on to address the internal barriers to cross selling which he rightly assesses as more significant than the external ones. Colleagues must share information about the client, trust one another not to steal that client and have an incentive to share success. If these can be satisfactorily addressed, then the cross-sales approach should adopt the techniques expounded in Chapter 5 and 6: except that this is now clearly a warm contact who can be approached with the best and easiest possible lead in 'I was talking to my colleague XYZ about your needs and he thought you would find our 123 service of value . . .'

Two particular 'extra' offers that should be considered in the context of the marketing plan for 'stroking' existing clients are seminars and training. Both are ideal for maintaining visibility, for enhancing reputation, and for giving the client something concrete to take away. The glory days of conspicuous corporate entertaining are gone and today clients usually want something tangible to justify (to boss and/or conscience) giving up their time to a supplier. A seminar on a relevant topic or training (basic or on the latest developments in a sector) will both satisfy this need. Conferences and exhibitions might also be considered.

Seminars should not be taken lightly, i.e. 'we know all about subject X so can pull a presentation together in no time at all'. Remember your actions are designed to enhance the agency's reputation and so care and attention, particularly preparation, should be taken. You might like to consider going for something grander such as a **conference**. This implies a major marketing effort and probably requires including speakers from outside your company. The best means of achieving success here is to co-sponsor with a company in a complementary sphere and get a professional conference organizer to arrange the event. This takes it out of the obvious sales arena, giving the occasion greater objectivity and impartiality while still enabling your own speakers prime sites. The conference organizer will, however, be motivated to achieve maximum attendance and so will employ many of the skills espoused in this book to achieve this end result, focusing on the topic as bait rather than your organization's participation. What you gain the right to is the vital attendance list, which will be your base for cold canvass after the event.

Seminar or conference – how to make it a success is the issue. It's not as easy as it seems. Once the date is fixed, it will happen, whether you are ready or not! Deadlines just have to be met. Planning is vital. So here is a checklist:

- *Choose the title with care.* It needs to offer something valuable, i.e. helpful, to the prospects. In other words, of the 'How to . . .' benefits-type rather than 'We can do . . .' feature-type.
- *Venue* – select on the basis of audience (type and size) and budget. Visit in advance. Ensure good audiovisual equipment, airy but no acres of wasted space, air conditioning, blackout facilities, quality of service from supplier. Think about signage, toilets, cloakroom facilities. Consider the backdrop – will you need set builders? Refreshments planning.
- Formal, well-produced *invitations* need to be sent out sufficiently far in advance. These should specify clearly the content and timings. Include travel instructions.
- Invitations to be followed up by telephone *reminders*.
- *Date* – choose with care. Avoid Mondays and Fridays. Miss national holidays. Provide sufficient advance warning (at least one month).
- A good geographic *location* should be chosen (easy to reach, overnight accommodation).
- *Timing* should be comfortable – ideally not a whole day for a seminar, rather 10.00 a.m. till 12.30 p.m. with a buffet lunch to follow.
- *Outside speakers* add credibility, especially if from the client side.
- On the day – have sufficient *support staff* on hand (do not underestimate); insist that speakers run through their slides; badges; message service for delegates; programmes.
- Copies of *lecture material* or notes to be available to take away.

In other words, if you're going to do it, at least do it properly. You want the event to be remembered – for the right reasons.

Exhibitions are growing in popularity as a standalone or add-on to conferences. The great appeal is a tightly focused and targeted audience. And another face-to-face opportunity to meet prospects. They provide a means of placing your organization on an almost equal footing with rivals, with only your stand as a discriminator. In assessing whether or not to participate, the first criterion is likely throughput of prospects. This is the be all and end all of a successful exhibition – numbers. So is it sponsored by sufficiently well-read media or high membership trade bodies, is the crucial question to ask. After that be prepared to fight hard for a good location with potential high traffic before you decide how much to invest in your stand itself. On the day(s), keep your staff outward facing – there is a terrible tendency for them to enjoy the opportunity for an out-of-office relaxing chat, turning their backs on the prospects passing.

Some tips regarding exhibitions (but equally relevant for conferences also) from Tim Harris in *Professional Marketing* (March 1994):

- 25 per cent of the work is planning; 25 per cent is attending; 50 per cent is following up the leads generated

- key elements are strategy; position; size/shape; design

strategy = having clear objectives – showcase? launch? niche target group?

position = study the floor plan; get a better position by signing up early

size and shape = biggest is not always best

design = vital; the aim is to offer your visitors the opportunity to see, compare, touch and discuss face to face; your stand is a representation of the public face of your firm – so go for quality

Turning next to **training**, this is a form of PR that you may feel capable of offering. The demand is enormous, since many of your clients will wish to keep in touch with your specialism and/or to use you to bring new and often young staff up to speed. But make no mistake – it is very time consuming of your executive resource. The training materials have to be prepared, checked off against participants' requirements, and then carried into action. Not everyone is a good trainer, and your organization's guru may have to hand over his lovingly prepared material to a more charismatic speaker.

The rewards of successful training are great. The gratitude of clients (both those attending and their seniors) is considerable. You may have converts for life. Word of mouth will spread the gospel further than you ever dreamed.

Questions on which you will have to make a decision include:

- Do you offer the course to a single company (invitation) or to any subscribers (open)?
- For single company courses – your place or theirs?
- For multi-company courses – any potential client attendance conflicts of the 'we didn't realize you were working for our competition also!' kind.
- Do you charge and, if so, how much?

Don't be too theoretical on this issue. Clients are keen to see your skills in action, and case studies are of equal interest as the lectures on the 'scientific' background.

Should this development prove popular and a catalogue of training materials and case studies built up, it may be possible to open another avenue of PR related to training. Can you offer to help your trade body with regard to training? What about the universities, colleges and business schools (particularly MBA courses)? These too are desperate for case study material that is up to date and relevant to real business situations. It can surely be no bad thing to put your name in front of impressionable students who sooner or later will become potential prospects or employees. But you must approach it profession-ally – a poor presentation with poor material and an obvious lack of preparation will have a negative effect. I would advise you strongly to spend quality time on teaching and lecturing – it is fun, it is valued highly, and it will undoubtedly provide a payback. I myself can point to major new business wins and excellent new employees, all of which resulted from appearances at business schools and trade body training sessions. This was only achieved after the investment of a considerable amount of my own time to develop customized material targeted to my audiences' needs – case studies, simulation exercises, explanatory hand-outs, etc.

Chapter 12

A view from the other side

Clients need to buy and therefore it should come as no surprise to learn that all the activities detailed in this book to date will work, if applied with dedication and skill. Don't expect many clients to acknowledge this fact – few are willing to admit to having been sold to. Most buyer surveys suggest that buying decisions are highly rational processes following elaborate scouting of the offers, the close study of learned articles, or the personal recommendation of respected colleagues or friends.

Occasionally the truth will out and some will confess to actually scanning their direct mail, being intrigued or seduced by a prospecting call, and responding to a piece of blatant but appealing PR. Because they know that to do their job well they must always remain open to new ideas. How else can one explain the many hundreds of important buyers who willingly put aside three days to isolate themselves with their worst enemies, the salespeople, at the annual marketing forum on the Canberra?

So what attracts a prospect to stop, look and listen? Here is an example of how NOT to do it:

> Once upon a time, a big professional firm asked its senior fee earners to visit their clients' offices at no charge, just to get to know them better. It was hoped that helping the fee earners learn more about their clients would lead to better advice, thereby further solidifying relationships and potentially leading to additional work in the same or a new area.
>
> One senior partner, after grudgingly agreeing to ask if the client would be interested in such a trip, was rebuffed. 'See, I told you it

wouldn't work!' he observed smugly to the marketing director. 'I called the client and offered to go and visit them to see where they could give me more work and they didn't even want me to come. I told you marketing doesn't work!'

Ross Fishman, *Professional Marketing*, November 1997

Rather let's listen to someone controlling a multi-million pound budget, who isolated seven approaches as appealing to him personally. They may be employed as part of a prospecting call, in a mailshot or as PR; it doesn't matter as long as it gets through to him. And he was willing to admit to receiving pitches from around two suppliers each week, though only as a result of an approach that caught his imagination.

- *A report on some original research*
  Who can resist! Free information on the subject that occupies most of his waking hours – he can't turn it down. But beware: it has to be new and relevant. He knows a lot about his market and it will be a good study that will tell him something he didn't already know. In particular, it must address the target group of interest to him. Obviously a key role here for PR and maybe also the possibility of some stylish company literature in which the material can be presented and circulated. Not ideal as a telephone prospection opening gambit – too easy for the target simply to ask you to put it in the post!
- *An in-depth analysis of his market*
  Again, something hard to turn down – but it had better be good, i.e. insightful. If it genuinely reveals your intellectual capability, then the benefits may be enormous for your future relationship. Agencies should remember that they know a little about a lot of markets; the prospect should know a lot about only his market – so it is not easy to surprise or impress him. PR and literature are the most suitable vehicles to carry this. But not the best tools for prospection.
- *Invitation to participate in research*
  Willingness to be a research respondent depends on a number of factors, but if the subject matter is directly relevant, if the results will be made available, and (for qualitative studies especially) if the fellow interviewees are peers in his sector, then likelihood of participation is enhanced. Everyone is flattered to have his opinions solicited, especially in his specialist sector.
- *Critique of his current activities*
  Obviously this goes straight to his heart – or even his guts! But, once again, you'd better be able to back it up! For a new arrival it may be a pleasure to gain supporting evidence on the failures of his predecessors; for an incumbent you may be killing his own baby. So tread carefully and be helpful with constructive rather than only destructive criticism.

- *Leaders in your own field*
  If you can truly substantiate such a claim then he should be listening to you and will find the offer of a meeting hard to resist. Use this device if it can work for you; but ...
  - make sure you are talking to the right person
  - don't drown the prospect in jargon just because you are the expert
  - don't just talk; listen to him as well
  Don't be too restrictive – you needn't be the biggest or best in the entire sector – it is sufficient to have that strength in a subsector or in a recognized specialism. And remember to stress the benefit of this quality and not just the feature itself if you are going to use the claim for prospection.
- *Famous personality*
  Every industry has its luminaries and those agencies that employ or are identified with them can take advantage of the ensuing fame and desire to rub shoulders with the great. But not at second hand. The contact should come directly from the 'star'. The building and maintenance of this fame is a task for which PR is excellent.
- *Exploiting uncertainty*
  Deep down within many clients there is the fear of exploitation: 'Am I being ripped off by agency X?', 'Who's paying for their glamorous new offices?', 'Why can't I properly check their fee structure?' It would take a saintly agency not to have the rare occasion of inside knowledge concerning a competitor's failure, weakness, key staff loss and possibly even impropriety – and be unwilling to exploit it. And it would take a very self-assured client to turn a deaf ear to the information.

So choose your weapons and move into the attack. Prospects are waiting for your call, and if it's not yours it will be your rival's. As confirmed here, clients are in business to buy, so if you've got something to sell you need to bring it – and you – to their attention.

The above just represents an individual view – it might be more sensible to gain a wider and more objective perspective on client needs. The next chapter deals with this subject.

Chapter 13

Researching your market

The definition of marketing provided at the start of Chapter 2 emphasized how it is based on 'identifying customer needs'. Market research provides the objective means of achieving this information. And you certainly must be armed with a clear understanding of these needs prior to building your marketing plan and before you go on the road cold canvassing.

I have hesitated before directly addressing the subject of market research, under the impression that you, the reader, may well have felt by now that, as a result of all my case studies showing the application of new business techniques being drawn from my own sphere of activity, you have already been subjected to more exposure to market research than you ever wished!

There are two additional good reasons for not ignoring this topic. First, the text has already, of necessity, had to refer to research at various stages because of its obvious relevance – Chapter 3, item 4, research as an integral part of marketing; Chapter 7, item 6, research as a PR device; Chapter 10, item 3, research for publication; Chapter 11, customer satisfaction measurement; Chapter 12, research participation as an incentive. Second, I am, of course, well qualified to advise on the benefits and pitfalls of using research. So here goes.

I will first address five main operational issues, which provide advice on the means research places at your disposal and the manner in which to apply them in order to gain the required information. These issues are . . .

1 research benefits and limitations
2 how to brief an agency and judge a proposal
3 DIY research
4 qualitative studies
5 quantitative studies

Then I will turn from the means to the end – what research can deliver. Knowledge of the client and his or her business is crucial to successful differentiation, so, in the professional services sector where so many firms claim to be committed to providing their clients with customized solutions, it is indeed surprising that their offers end up being so similar. To avoid this and to succeed in differentiating yourself, market research is required to allow your organization to win new business. It is also vital to get regular feedback as to how your organization is perceived, how its performance has been evaluated, and how this fits into the competitive scene. You may want to address via research the following:

- Segmentation/specialization – define and segment your marketplace in terms of the needs, behaviour and attitudes of your clients. Then you can decide on whether you need to offer 'different strokes for different folks' or can you be all things to all clients?
- Image – what is yours? How does it stack up against your competition? Are you seen as an integrated organization with common values? This information will form the basis for your promotional strategy planning.
- Pricing – are you seen as a commodity or premium supplier?
- Service – basic or added value? Customer satisfaction measurement should be an essential element of your information base.

. . . and combined together my information on means and ends should help you to start on your way down the research road.

1 Research benefits and limitations

Research is like a lamp-post – it should be used for illumination rather than support. It is not a crutch but one of many inputs into your strategy and assessment. It can offer risk reduction through the benefit of its objectivity. But if conducted without sufficient professionalism, time or money, it can be positively misleading and hence dangerous. Research is a social science and is surrounded by error – sample bias (are all potential respondents given the opportunity to be selected for interview?), measurement bias (are the questions put in an unbiased manner?), sample error (is your sample size large enough to reduce statistical variability to the minimum?). All research-derived figures must be seen as having a plus or minus range around them.

2 How to brief an agency and judge a proposal

A good briefing of a market research agency in which you make them fully aware of the marketing background to your situation is crucial. Here is a checklist of the information you should provide:

BACKGROUND
OBJECTIVES

POSSIBLE METHOD e.g. qualitative or quantitative (see below), face to face or telephone or postal?
RESPONDENTS FOR INTERVIEW e.g. clients? prospects?
PENETRATION OF RESPONDENTS – how easy to find (will you provide a listing?)
MATERIALS – to be supplied by you (e.g. test advertisements)
TIMING
BUDGET (optional whether or not you decide to reveal this)

When you receive the agency's response (proposal) you should evaluate it on the following criteria – does it address these eight issues:

1 WHY – does the agency understanding the background to the research?
2 HOW – what method of data collection will be used
3 WHO – the definition of the respondent selection criteria
4 HOW MANY – sample size
5 WHERE – the geographic spread of the interviewing
6 WHAT – an outline of the questions to be asked
7 WHEN – timing
8 HOW MUCH – cost

3 DIY research

The above criteria can guide you if you wish to hire an outside agency to conduct the research. What if you want to tackle it in-house. Don't underestimate the time and effort required: most organizations are not set up to handle the volumes of paper, post, checking and data preparation/ processing that may be involved when dealing with hundreds or thousands of interviews. Key steps on the research path are provided here as a checklist for you:

● Define your sample, its size and selection method
● Choose your data collection method (face to face/telephone/post)
● Design your questionnaire
● Collect your data
● Clean your data
● Enter your data into the computer and define analyses required
● Interpret and report on your data

There is an intermediate solution available. The rapid growth of the research industry has spawned a range of small agencies offering 'field and tab' services (see Market Research Society Organizations Book, tel: London 0171 490 4911). These can offer you assistance in those areas where too much of your time and effort could otherwise be wasted (i.e. data collection and data preparation/ processing) leaving you still to control the design of the study and interpretation of results.

4 Qualitative studies

Focus groups (around eight participants) or individual 'depth' interviews (one on one) are the main tools of the qualitative researcher. This is non-statistical, small-scale, non-directive research conducted without a questionnaire and often lasting up to two hours. The research moderator is skilled at focusing the interview on the required subject matter in a gentle, probing manner. The aim is to get beneath the rational 'skin' of the respondent reaching the more psychological motivations and needs. You may sometimes be able to watch the interview via closed circuit TV or via a one-way mirror. The researcher analyses the recordings before reporting on the findings. Very good at presenting the full range of possible views in a market but based on small samples, so indicative rather than conclusive.

5 Quantitative studies

While qualitative research provides a feel for the 'range' of behaviour and attitudes that exist, quantitative measures their 'extent'. It does this via questionnaire-based research with sample sizes generally exceeding 100 and often over 1000. Statistical analysis is possible. The questionnaire should be designed like a funnel – starting with very broad-based questions and moving gradually towards the more detailed. Only from the latter should the respondent be able to deduce the survey's sponsor, so that the earlier questions are unbiased (this does not apply to self-completion postal questionnaires, obviously). The questions may be 'closed' (i.e. pre-coded, the potential responses already listed) or 'open' (i.e. verbatim recording of respondents' answers). Face to face is the most expensive and time consuming data collection option, but offers the opportunity for a lengthy interview; telephone is more efficient but is probably limited to around twenty minutes; postal methods suffer from poor response rates but are cheap.

Turning from the means to the end:

1 Market studies

Designed to provide a two-way view onto your market – for you to understand your clients, and for them to tell you how they assess your organization.

In the former case, your ambition may extend to a wish to size the total market and determine your market share. More likely you will restrict yourself to gaining an understanding of how decisions are made and who makes them.

How do clients in your sector gather information/opinions on suppliers? What is their decision-making unit? How and where do they spend their budget? You will want to identify their judgement criteria in the selection of suppliers and establish their relative importance.

In the second case, the focus turns onto you and your competitors – what is the level of awareness (spontaneous/prompted) among clients of all 'brands' and marketing activities, who would be considered for tenders, what are 'brand images' – how are you rated, overall and on specific attributes.

Such a study usually begins with qualitative investigation and then moves into quantitative measurement. The qualitative most probably will involve a small number (5–20) of individual depth interviews with key representatives of the client base. It aims to gain a deep insight into your marketplace and ensure that all relevant aspects are included in the next stage. The quantitative follow-up will then best be carried out on the telephone among a representative sample (at least 100), ensuring stratification so that major key players are not missed, and possibly boosted in numbers to reflect their buying power. The data analysis should aim to look for homogeneous client subgroups which can be targeted via tailored sales and marketing activities, e.g. the 'price buyers', the 'quality seekers', the 'big name buyers', the 'technophiles', etc.

2 Pricing research

Aimed at gaining an understanding of your price elasticity and to provide a demand curve of price against purchase likelihood. Price and/or value will certainly already have been one of the attributes assessed as part of the image study above. There may be an additional need to subject it to a more detailed analysis – taking a specific, hypothetical brief as a basis for the evaluation. At what price would a bid be rejected as too expensive, at what price would it be regarded as suspiciously cheap, etc?

A trade-off exercise where price is evaluated as one of a range of service elements could provide a further valuable insight into your future pricing strategy.

3 Customer satisfaction measurement

Usually conducted as quantitative studies using postal methods. A distinction needs to be drawn between occasional strategic studies designed to identify client needs, and operational studies aimed at tracking your performance on a regular basis. The former are likely to be more comprehensive, since they must stand alone as a guide for strategic decision making and also act as a database for future reference. The latter are required to provide trend data. In this situation also it may be possible to conduct a census rather than a sampling exercise, since questionnaires can be despatched following each and every project conducted, indeed ISO registration may demand it.

'How Market Research is Stealing into Legal Circles'

This headline appeared in the December 1997 issue of *Research* magazine, the monthly trade journal of the UK Market Research Society. It shows how research has now entered the ultimate professional services bastion, the legal profession, and therefore represents just the trend towards using marketing services professionally which this book aims at promoting. So I quote liberally from the article.

> Gone are the days when the only research reports to be found on a lawyer's desk were the testimonies of expert witnesses. Today, you are just as likely to find senior partners from a top twenty city law firm sitting through a full-scale presentation of qualitative research on their clients' reactions to a proposed merger with a leading management consultancy.
>
> IFF Research, which recently completed that particular task, is one of a small but growing band of research suppliers trying to get a handle on an arcane world with no history of professional marketing or research.
>
> 'A number of partners will invariably be completely cynical at the outset', Jules Hall, a Director of IFF explains. 'The problem is they think they know all there is to know about their clients.'
>
> Though lawyers are behind accountancy firms in terms of research literacy, the feeling among suppliers is that, thanks to recession, deregulation and – long after the rest of industry – the rise of a legal customer care culture, the legal profession has become a reluctant research, and research agency, convert.
>
> Legal firms, like research agencies, are having to manage the globalisation of their sector while fighting off home front challenges from other professional services ... As Tom Rose, one of a team of business developers for Clifford Chance, puts it: 'Partners are having to become research literate. It isn't an option, it's a necessity'.
>
> The Law Society's press officer, David McNeill, debunks the myth of lawyers as a pinstriped elite doing business by gentlemen's agreements. 'The Society's view is that if you want to thrive you have to adopt proper business practice and that includes marketing and market research. Firms are successful for a reason – they've got their marketing and research right and fight tooth and nail for business.'
>
> ... The barriers – if that is what they are – are largely structural. Law firms are organized as partnerships who are specialist lawyers working on a fee-earning treadmill and often slow to appreciate the skills of other disciplines.

... 'legal partners throw up their hands in horror when we suggest talking to clients. It's the confidentiality issue but also the image of them carrying out research. We try and explain that clients are usually impressed that law firms are tackling issues in such a professional way', Roger Stubbs, MORI. MORI's high media profile helped it win a perceptions study of the legal market for Bristol-based Osborne Clark, a 45-partner firm specialising in bringing companies to the Stock Market, who then used the findings for PR purposes. The law firm is one of several buying into MORI's Captains of Industry perceptions survey.

The good news for other (research) agencies is the emergence of a new cadre of legal Business Development Directors, mainly from non-legal backgrounds, who may champion research internally. One of them is Philip Hall, business development director at Withers, a City firm specialising in family law. After seven years as an account director at Ogilvy & Mather, he switched disciplines and brought with him a knowledge and appreciation of research tools. He promptly commissioned a branding and positioning study from DVL Smith, who talked to clients and professional contacts in the accountancy and stockbroking world, as well as internal partners.

Osborne Clarke has taken research to even further lengths. It claims to have overturned its fee-earning philosophy as a result of an annual client satisfaction survey. 'For me it's the firm's single most important management tool,' Leslie Perrin says. 'We've placed client service in a completely different part of our people's consciousness since we started doing it.'

'The first survey was a bombshell, really. We were good at the soft skills, things we used to agonise about – for instance, clients regarded us as easy to do business with and responsive, but not so good on the hard, process issues, like billing, deadlines, delivering the same level of service across the firm and keeping clients in touch with major developments. Since then we've worked hard on these factors.'

The bulk of legal research work so far has centred on client satisfaction and PR, but more ambitious projects, like strategic development and policy work, are becoming commonplace. Solicitors have become increasingly interested in international aspects, observes Dermot Cox.

Chapter 14

Next steps – Putting the skills into practice

There's nothing for it now – you've come this far; it's time to put the theory into practice. It's time for you to go out and win new business for yourself. We can use this final section as a review and an *aide-mémoire* using a hypothetical new business example, also answering any remaining doubts, queries and questions at the end of the chapter. Our framework will be the 'Twenty Golden Rules' and the 'Push/Pull' dichotomy of Chapters 3 and 4, respectively, and our key words will be 'marketing' and 'planning', as we complete the following matrix structure:

	Plan	Target	Tools
Marketing strategy			
Tactical conclusions			
Action plan			

The vertical axis is designed to guide you into making the translation from theoretical strategy (at the top), via practical measures to execution (at the base). The horizontal axis reminds you of the key considerations at each stage of the vertical scale – from ends (on the left), via your audience, to the means (on the right).

Let us consider a virtual professional service organization – but please be prepared to replace my suggestion with details of your own company. Mine is called The Micro Training Consultancy (TMTC), a five-partner operation that offers training in the use of direct marketing to marketing companies. All the partners have worked in both client-side and agency functions involving a focus on direct marketing, and they have developed a computer simulation program, MicroLaunch, that allows rival teams of training course participants the opportunity to try their hands at applying a series of direct marketing actions during the launch of a new product, attempting to achieve maximum sales. TMTC believe that there is a need within companies for their staff to become more knowledgeable and skilled in the application of direct marketing. They know that the simulation exercise provides vital practical education in a stimulating and participative environment.

Step 1 is for the partners to decide the crucial elements of a marketing strategy upon which they must agree. This produces the first line below.

	Plan	Target	Tools
Marketing strategy	Mission USP Brand values	Marketing companies	Demonstration Media
Tactical conclusions			
Action plan			

Then the partners need to flesh out the contents of this strategy – 'where's the beef?' – what is the mission? What is their brand and what does it offer? Who are their target audiences? How can this all be translated into sales and marketing executions? The matrix now develops further, completing line 2:

	Plan	Target	Tools
Marketing strategy	Mission USP Brand values	Marketing companies	Demonstration Media
Tactical conclusions	'We provide the essential training for all users of direct marketing'; 'We are the only training agency focusing on the needs of users'; Staffed by experts all with agency-side experience; MicroLaunch – a unique training simulation	Marketing and human resources directors have the need to train their marketing staff	Develop a prospection script for cold canvass demonstrations; plan advertising and direct executions; think about PR devices
Action plan			

The target group is clearly defined, TMTC know what their USP is (key words – 'essential training'/'focus on the needs of users'/'unique Microlaunch simulation'), and it is obvious that cold canvass is the way to make the whole offer tangible.

Now we have something that can be converted into a cold canvass pitch and into a marketing execution. The latter should involve outside experts, though we can already hypothesize about possible activities (see below). The prospection script for cold canvass appointments is clear (an accompanying objections list will be customized for TMTC.)

> Good morning/afternoon, Mr/Mrs ... My name is ... and I'm Senior Partner at The Micro Training Consultancy; are you familiar with our Consultancy?
>
> ...
>
> Then, you'll know/Then, I can tell you – we are specialists in training marketing practitioners like you in the skills of direct marketing using our own MicroLaunch simulation game which allows participants to test their knowledge against a computer program ... and I'd like to come and demonstrate it for you because I believe it

could be of considerable value to you and your company for your staff to develop these skills. Tell me Mr/Mrs ..., do ... or ... suit you better?

Fine, how would a ... next week suit you? How about at ... or perhaps a little later in the day?

Fine, so that's ... o'clock, on ... day the ... of this month.

Thank you very much, Mr/Mrs ... I'll write to confirm that and I look forward to meeting you then. Goodbye.

The advertising and direct marketing will feature the Microlaunch simulation, majoring on the risk-free benefit it offers for participants to apply their training in a laboratory situation, without spending real money. Both media will offer a free disk with a sample of the simulation programme. The target audience will be reached by using marketing human resource magazines, including those focusing on direct marketing and advertising.

	Plan	*Target*	*Tools*
Marketing strategy	Mission USP Brand values	Marketing companies	Demonstration Media
Tactical conclusions	Essential for users Microlaunch	Marketing and HR directors	Prospection; Canvass PR
Action plan	Maintain focus on users not agency personnel	Marketing and HR magazines	Start prospection; launch response ads/ direct mail with free disk; PR – invite journalist to attend training session to see MicroLaunch

In brief, that's my 'winning new business' programme put into place for TMTC, hopefully illuminating the integration of all the elements described in this book via a hypothetical example. Many extra embellishments can be added to enhance its sophistication, but the key principles remain. Why not try the same exercise with your own organization?

Questions and Answers

But before sending you off to put all the above into practice, let me address a few final difficult questions that have been thrown at me over the years regarding my sales and marketing principles, and provide you with what I feel to be the best available answers to what are sometimes issues without unequivocal solutions.

Q. Can't I delegate the prospection task to my assistant to do on my behalf?

A. No. Your assistant is not the senior, experienced professional expert that you are, and cannot pretend to be. The task is yours: delegation is simply an excuse motivated by fear and/or snobbery rather than having any rational basis.

Q. I really can't see myself using that script of yours, it's just not me

A. I have always allowed you to modify, as long as you adhere to the basic principles and the underlying logic. These are necessary not for any dogmatic reasons, but because they enhance your chance of success.

Q. Have you ever called prospects on their mobile phones?

A. No, I haven't and I would be hesitant to do so, given that you may be regarded as intruding on their private time.

Q. I can think of some more possible objections beyond those you've listed which are particularly applicable to my sector.

A. No problem. Address them using the principles enunciated – ride over the objection without engaging in an argument and then return to your close, attempting to gain an appointment

Q. Let's assume that more and more professionals read your book and put your theories into practice – won't it be self-defeating, as the volume of calls multiplies and the prospects are taught how to deflect them?

A. Well, first of all, this is an assumption. But let's take it step by step. If the popularity of my 'Winning New Business' technique increases, it will be because it works; so you'd better join the game right now. Of course, nothing remains static, and we may indeed find prospects raising their defensive skills. Our job then will be to adapt our own methods – and the cycle of attack and counter will continue. But I think we can always assume that a part of our weaponry will pierce the defensive armour and get us through to win business, because our services are necessary. So 'just do it'.

Index